Ambrose / Harris

FORMAT

n. the shape and
size of a book etc.

Academia
the environment of learning

AVA Publishing SA
Switzerland

An AVA Book

Published by AVA Publishing SA

Rue des Fontenailles 16, Case postale,

1000 Lausanne 6, Switzerland

Tel: +41 786 005 109 Email: enquiries@avabooks.ch

Distributed by Thames and Hudson (ex-North America)

181a High Holborn, London WC1V 7QX, United Kingdom

Tel: +44 20 7845 5000 Fax: +44 20 7845 5055

Email: sales@thameshudson.co.uk

www.thamesandhudson.com

Distributed in the USA & Canada by:

Watson-Guptill Publications

770 Broadway

New York, New York 10003

Tel: 1 800 451 1741

Email: info@wgpub.com

www.wgpub.com

English Language Support Office

AVA Publishing (UK) Ltd.

Tel: +44 1903 204 455 Email: enquiries@avabooks.co.uk

ISBN 2-940373-28-0

10 9 8 7 6 5 4 3

Design and text by Gavin Ambrose and Paul Harris

Original photography by Xavier Young

www.xavieryoung.co.uk

Original book and series concept devised by Natalia Price-Cabrera

Production and separations by AVA Book Production Pte. Ltd., Singapore

Tel: +65 6334 8173 Fax: +65 6334 0752 Email: production@avabooks.com.sg

Format

R Newbold

This brochure for a clothing range by R Newbold, designed by Aboud Sodano, is a 42-page section printed in four special colours – black, silver, blue and yellow – rather than the normal process colours. All the images appear as duotones of silver and black. Bound into a hard cover there is a die cut which has removed a large square from one corner to create a uniquely shaped publication.

Client: R Newbold
Design: Aboud Sodano
Process: 42-page section, four special colours litho, hard cover, die cut

Contents

Rose Design

Tank

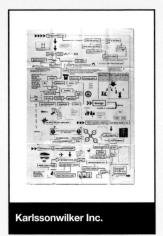

Karlssonwilker Inc.

MadeThought

Why Not Associates

Research Studios

Introduction

Modern design practice has a multitude of tools at its disposal with which it can create printed matter that effectively communicates. Layout, typography, colour and images are all critical in differentiating one design from another and relaying information, but an often underrated and underused tool is that of the format itself, the physical presence of the piece.

Format is often overlooked because of its almost exclusively utilitarian nature. This, and the existence of many generic formats, means that format is something that many designers do not realise they are thinking about. The format provides a physical point of contact with the user that affects how we receive the printed and on-line communication.

We are familiar with a wide range of formats, mainly for ergonomic reasons: a poster needs to be large enough to be read from a distance; a stamp needs to be small enough to fit on an envelope; a book needs to be large enough for text to print at a readable size, but small enough to be held comfortably in the hand.

Although printed matter is often predisposed to be of a certain size, shape, extent and weight, designers often use format to vary these and add an extra dimension to their work.

The Book
Book formats serve a range of functions, from being comfortable to hold by hand, to being on a lectern; and books have different anticipated lifespans, from paperback to hardback.

The Magazine
Some of the most impressive design in the 20th century centred around magazine design, a field that continues to innovate. While the majority are of standard format, there are exceptions.

The Poster
Posters come in various shapes and sizes. Some are rarely viewed close up and represent some of the largest scale print work. The examples presented here are on a smaller scale and generally folded such as poster-wrapped books.

The Object
Objects can be mailers, invitations, tickets, menus and other printed matter, many of which have to quickly grab attention and therefore often result in some of the most unusual and distinctive formats from the simple to the elaborate.

The Screen
Onscreen formats do not need to be restricted by screen dimensions. The designer can use a variety of techniques to creatively use space such as pop-up boxes, animations and innovative navigation.

The Brochure
Although often in similar formats as small books or magazines, the intention is quite different: brochures inform and try to solicit positive responses to their contents.

Client: Stockport Arts
and Health
Design: Eg.G
Process: Half-Canadian
binding

Lost Found Time
This collection of poetry by senior citizens that recounts some of their experiences
designed by Eg.G for Stockport Arts and Health uses a half-Canadian binding.

How to get the most out of this book

This book introduces different aspects of format design via dedicated chapters for each topic. Each chapter provides numerous examples of creative format use in design from leading contemporary design studios, annotated to explain the reasons behind the design choices made.

Key design principles are isolated so that the reader can see how they are applied in practice.

Clear navigation

Each chapter has a clear strapline to allow readers to quickly locate areas of interest.

Visual explanations

Design theory is combined with commercial design projects to show readers how it was achieved.

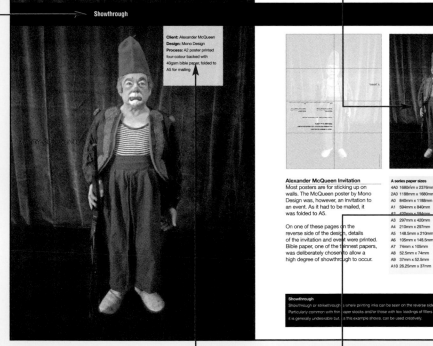

Showthrough

50 **51**

Client: Alexander McQueen
Design: Mono Design
Process: A2 poster printed four-colour backed with 40gsm bible paper, folded to A5 for mailing

Alexander McQueen Invitation
Most posters are for sticking up on walls. The McQueen poster by Mono Design was, however, an invitation to an event. As it had to be mailed, it was folded to A5.

On one of these pages on the reverse side of the design, details of the invitation and event were printed. Bible paper, one of the thinnest papers, was deliberately chosen to allow a high degree of showthrough to occur.

A series paper sizes
4A0	1680mm x 2376mm
2A0	1188mm x 1680mm
A0	840mm x 1188mm
A1	594mm x 840mm
A2	420mm x 594mm
A3	297mm x 420mm
A4	210mm x 297mm
A5	148.5mm x 210mm
A6	105mm x 148.5mm
A7	74mm x 105mm
A8	52.5mm x 74mm
A9	37mm x 52.5mm
A10	26.25mm x 37mm

Showthrough
Showthrough or strikethrough is where printing inks can be seen on the reverse side of the page. Particularly common with thin paper stocks and/or those with low loadings of fillers and coating, it is generally undesirable but, as this example shows, can be used creatively.

Format Showthrough

Additional information

Paper stocks, weights, bindings, client, designers and other points of interest are included.

Technical information

Design theory and terminology is decoded to foster greater understanding of design concepts.

Format How to get the most out of this book

Introductions
Special section introductions outline basic concepts that will be discussed.

Written explanations
Key points are explained within the context of an example project.

Examples
Commercial projects from contemporary designers bring the principles under discussion alive.

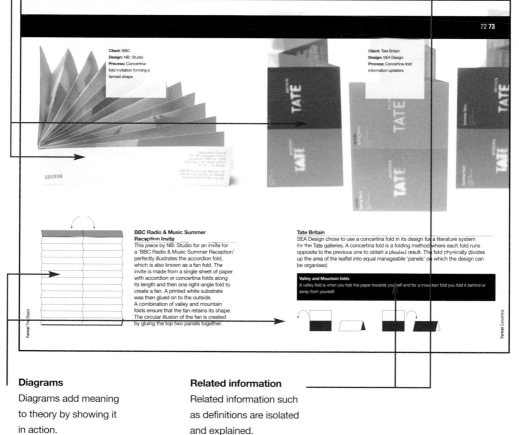

Diagrams
Diagrams add meaning to theory by showing it in action.

Related information
Related information such as definitions are isolated and explained.

Format How to get the most out of this book

The Book

Client: Sculpture at Goodwood
Design: MadeThought
Process: 48- and 176-page books connected by z-bind cover. Foil-blocked outer cover

The Book

A book is a means of organising and presenting many pieces of information in one package. Whether compiling related vignettes, applying a sequential order or collating otherwise random pieces of information, books become a sum of their parts.

Book format considerations include the nature and quantity of information to be presented, the anticipated lifetime of the product, and of course the perennial factors of target audience and cost. These affect choices such as stock selection, size, and print finishing. For example, colour graphics need higher quality paper stocks to reproduce a good image; and to ensure a long lifetime, a higher quality paper stock, durable binding and hard cover will be needed.

In contrast, paperbacks are generally produced in standard sizes as cheaply as possible on low quality pulp stock. Publishers spend their money on creating attractive covers to entice the customer, perhaps with foil blocking and embossing; quite a change from the days when books were produced without covers and people had to bind them themselves.

Choosing paper size and stock provides a starting point for a project, though there are many opportunities for creative departure through print finishing techniques, where elements are combined to produce unique and innovative designs.

Thinking Big – Sculpture at Goodwood (left)

Z-binds are used in several of the projects in this book, but here is an interesting application by MadeThought for client Sculpture at Goodwood. The publication is entitled *Thinking Big, Concepts for Twenty-first Century British Sculpture* with works from many leading sculptors including Tony Cragg, Jon Buck, Andy Goldsworthy et al. The book comprises two parts: the front section contains detailed biographies of the sculptors that created the 85 works, while the back section contains atmospheric and abstract imagery by Richard Learoyd. The unique aspect of this design is that the two sections share a z-fold cover that both separates and unites the two halves.

9 Kean Street

This brochure for Millennium Loft's 9 Kean Street development designed by Cartlidge Levene is a two-section publication connected by a perforated z-bind.

The front section uses the strong colour photography of Covent Garden by Gueorgui Pinkhassov, who was commissioned by the client to spend a week in Covent Garden to photograph the area. The back section has a more limited colour palette and contains information specific to the 22 lofts that comprise the development.

Client: Millennium Lofts
Design: Cartlidge Levene
Process: 44- and 32-page brochures connected with perforated z-bind cover

9 Kean Street
Covent Garden
22 Lofts

Client: Black Dog Publishing
Design: Society
Process: Single-colour litho with silk-screened greyboard cover and endpapers with buckram binding

City Racing

For this book, *City Racing, The Life and Times of an Artist-Run Gallery*, Society chose a greyboard cover to add grittiness to the publication and reflect its content. The cover and the endpapers were silk-screened and a green buckram binding applied.

Greyboard
Greyboard is packaging material made entirely from waste paper that can be lined or unlined.

Buckram
A coarse linen or cotton fabric sized with glue or gum used for covering a hard cover binding.

Standard paper uses

Paper type	Notes	Primary uses
Newsprint	Paper made primarily of mechanically ground wood pulp, shorter lifespan than other papers, cheap to produce, least expensive paper that can withstand normal printing processes.	Newspapers, comics.
Antique	Roughest finish offered on offset paper.	To add texture to publications such as annual reports.
Uncoated woodfree	Largest printing and writing paper category by capacity that includes almost all office and offset grades used for general commercial printing.	Office paper (printer and photocopy paper, stationery).
Mechanical	Produced using wood pulp, contains acidic lignins. Suitable for short-term uses as it will 'yellow' and colours will fade.	Newspapers, directories.
Art board	Uncoated board.	Cover stock.
Art	A high-quality paper with a clay filler to give a good printing surface, especially for halftones where definition and detail are important. Has high brightness and gloss.	Colour printing, magazines.
Cast coated	Coated paper with a high-gloss finish obtained while the wet coated paper is pressed or cast against a polished, hot, metal drum.	High-quality colour printing.
Chromo	A waterproof coating on a single side intended for good embossing and varnishing performance.	Labels, wrappings, and covers.
Cartridge	A thick white paper particularly used for pencil and ink drawings.	To add texture to publications such as annual reports.
Greyboard	Lined or unlined board made from waste paper.	Packaging material.
Flock	Paper coated with flock; very fine woollen refuse or vegetable fibre dust to give a velvety or cloth-like appearance.	Decorative covers.

Client: Nigel Coates /
Laurence King
Design: Why Not Associates
Process: 408-page book,
edition bound, multiple
page markers, foil-blocked
cover and bellyband

Ecstacity

Why Not Associates made a subtle and useful format enhancement in its design for architect Nigel Coates' book *Ecstacity* – which explores the dynamics of the city – by including several coloured page marker bands. Implying the need to mark several pages, the markers highlight and remind us of the complex multiplicity of the information contained within this book.

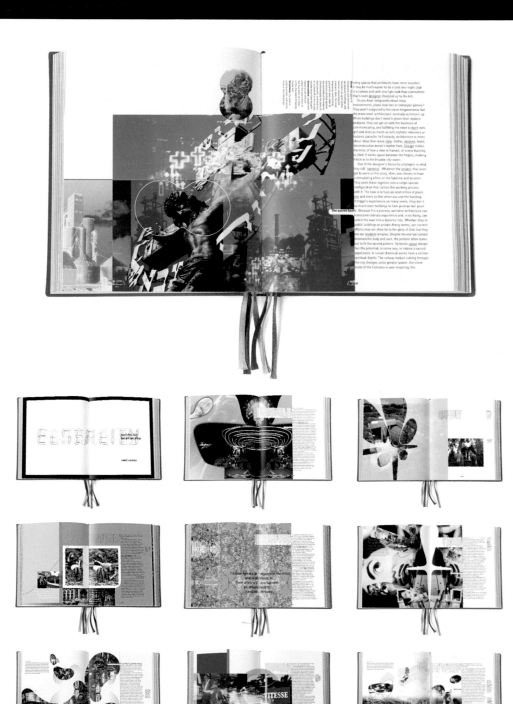

Client: Taylor &
Francis Routledge
Design: Gavin Ambrose
Process: One-colour litho
wrapped cover

ernö goldfinger – the life of an architect

nigel warburton

Ernö Goldfinger – The Life of an Architect

There are a surprising variety of standard book formats, as the table opposite shows.
The cover above shows the architect, Ernö Goldfinger, in front of Trellick Tower in
West London, which he designed, photographed by Peter Hamilton.

Book formats

Two main factors affect the final size of a page in a book: the size of the original sheet of paper, and the number of times the sheet of paper is folded before trimming. 'Folio editions' refers to books made of signatures that have been folded only once. 'Quarto editions' are formed from signatures folded twice (making four leaves or eight pages), and 'Octavo editions' are bound from signatures folded three times (making eight leaves or 16 pages). These book sizes were originally based around standard paper sizes, and represent a mathematical portion of a sheet of paper.

Bound book sizes			
Demy 16mo	143mm x 111mm	Imperial 8vo	279mm x 191mm
Demy 18mo	146mm x 95mm	Foolscap Quarto (4to)	216mm x 171mm
Foolscap Octavo (8vo)	171mm x 108mm	Crown 4to	254mm x 191mm
Crown (8vo)	191mm x 127mm	Demy 4to	260mm x 222mm
Large Crown 8vo	203mm x 133mm	Royal 4to	318mm x 254mm
Demy 8vo	222mm x 143mm	Imperial 4to	381mm x 279mm
Medium 8vo	241mm x 152mm	Crown Folio	381mm x 254mm
Royal 8vo	254mm x 159mm	Demy Folio	445mm x 286mm
Super Royal 8vo	260mm x 175mm	Royal Folio	508mm x 318mm
		Music	356mm x 260mm

Format Book formats

Dual artwork

Rather than creating different artworks for the two sizes of publication, a single artwork is output at different percentages. Separate covers are then applied giving the illusion of two very different publications. Artwork is typically reduced by 71% so that it can be changed from A3 format to A4. However, due to the unusual sized format of this book, the artwork was reduced to 58% so that it could migrate from 12in to 7in (304mm to 178mm).

DJs by Lopez

For a book about DJs featuring the photographs of Chris Lopez, Mono Design turned for inspiration to two key numbers close to the heart of any DJ to select two formats for the book: 7 and 12. These sizes correspond to the inch size of vinyl records used by DJs. The only difference between the books is scale; the pictures and text in one are larger than in the other. The change in scale in this instance does not affect the clarity or effect of the design, though this may not always be the case. Care needs to be taken to ensure that the larger of the two sizes doesn't appear clunky, and the smaller version become illegible.

A3 to A4 = 71% reduction

Legibility

Legibility

Legibility

Legibility

Client: AAPPL
Design: Mono Design
Process: Two different sized books, one edition bound the other perfect bound

dj's by lopez

Colin, Chris Coco, Cirilli Liberalist, Christian Smith, CJ Mak, Coldcut, Colin Dale, Danny Howells, Danny Rampling, Dave Angel, Dave Lee, DJ Cam, D.D DJ Disciple, DJ Yellorum, DJ Elari, DJ Elari Dieter, DJ Elik Morris, DJ Alonso, DJ Fabri, Chris A. Neil Tom, Fine Squad, Gilles Peterson, Grade, A Man Called Adam, Graeme A Man Called Adam, Alan Thompson, Alan of Aleks, Ali & Alison, Alison Woods.

dj's by lopez   AAPPL   Portrait photography of international dj's by Chris Lopez.   ◄STEREO►

dj's by lopez

Types of binding

Client: Struktur
Design: Struktur
Process: Two 32-page
saddle-stitched sections,
one eight-panel folded
cover, one elastic band

Hours Book

A binding method is generally selected for
the functional purpose it serves, but in Struktur's *Hours*
book it is used to make a physical separation in the
work. Half the book is a calendar of hours
while the other half comprises paintings by
an artist created within a certain amount of time.
They get quicker as the minutes disappear. Each part
is produced as a separate book and then bound
together by an elastic band, perhaps suggesting
the elasticity of time.

Tank Pages 44–45

KesselsKramer Page 167

Tank Page 95

Perfect binding

A binding method commonly used for paperback books where the signatures are held together with a flexible adhesive that also attaches a paper cover to the spine. The fore edge is trimmed flat.

Saddle-stitch

A binding method used for booklets, programmes and small catalogues. Signatures are nested and wire stitches are applied through the spine along the centrefold. When opened, saddle-stitched books lay flat.

Wiro / comb binding

A spine of metal (wiro) or plastic (comb) rings that binds and allows a document to open flat. Used for reports, office publications, manuals and so on. Usually with a hard cover stock.

North Pages 122–123

Eg.G Page 7

Eg.G Page 156

French fold

A sheet of paper that has two right-angle folds to form a four-page, uncut section. The section is sewn through the fold while the top edges remain folded and untrimmed. It's common for the inner reveals to be printed with a flood colour.

Canadian / half-Canadian binding

A spiral-bound volume with a wraparound cover that gives the benefits of spiral binding (lays flat, pages can be folded around) with the professional look of perfect binding. Half-Canadian has an exposed spine, a full Canadian has a covered spine.

Japanese or stab binding

A binding method whereby the pages are sewn together with one continual thread. Pages do not open flat. This is a very decorative binding method, not commonly used, but very luxurious.

Format Types of binding

Imposition and multiple stocks

With a simple four-colour job, imposition is not important as every page prints with the same four process colours. If you have the budget or the opportunity to alter the colour fall, however, such as by using a special colour or spot varnish, more intricate planning may be necessary. You will need to know which pages are to carry the spot colour by means of an imposition plan.

An imposition plan provides an economic benefit by reducing the number of sections that you need to print with the special colour. This plan also allows you to maximise the coverage of a special, for example pages 130, 131, 134, 135, 138, 139, 142 and 143 of this book all print with an additional fifth colour, Pantone 877 metallic. On an imposition plan these would all fall on the same side of one 16-page section.

Imposition is a visual representation or guide of how a publication will print.

This book prints to the imposition plan shown below. As it's bound in 16-page sections there are eight pages to view i.e. eight pages on each side of the sheet. It is specified as a 176-page book with a six-panel gatefold.

1	2	3	4	5	6	7	8	9	10	11	12	13	14	15	16
17	18	19	20	21	22	23	24	25	26	27	28	29	30	31	32
33	34	35	36	37	38	39	40	41	42	43	44	45	46	47	48

Three four-colour 16-page sections.

If you open a book, page 1 obviously backs-up with page 2, page 3 with 4, page 5 with 6 etc. When specifying colour fall remember this and it should be straightforward. In the first 16-page section above, pages 1, 4, 5, 8, 9, 12, 13 and 16 print together, with the remaining pages printing on the reverse. This means that these two groups of eight pages can be treated separately as shown in section nine below, printed in a special.

Tip-ins are normally spliced between sections. This six-panel tip-in falls between pages 48 and 49. It could however fall between any of the sections in this book.

Six-panel tip-in.

49	50	51	52	53	54	55	56	57	58	59	60	61	62	63	64
65	66	67	68	69	70	71	72	73	74	75	76	77	78	79	80
81	82	83	84	85	86	87	88	89	90	91	92	93	94	95	96
97	98	99	100	101	102	103	104	105	106	107	108	109	110	111	112
113	114	115	116	117	118	119	120	121	122	123	124	125	126	127	128
129	130	131	132	133	134	135	136	137	138	139	140	141	142	143	144
145	146	147	148	149	150	151	152	153	154	155	156	157	158	159	160

Seven four-colour 16-page sections.

A special colour has been applied to the highlighted pages in the ninth section. As the sections are printed eight-to-view these all fall on one side of a section.

161	162	163	164	165	166	167	168	169	170	171	172	173	174	175	176

Single-colour 16-page section printed on Kraft paper.

Format Imposition and multiple stocks

The diagrams below show an imposition plan a printer would specify for a job bound in 16-page sections; hence it has 16 pages across and will print 32 to a sheet (including the reverse of the 16 pages). As a book is printed in sections the colour blocks don't need to be next to each other as the job sections can be printed, cut, rearranged and bound.

96-page job with 48 pages printing colour and 48 pages printing single colour

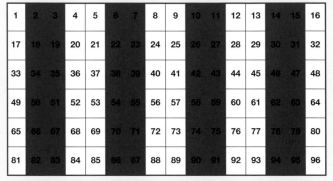

1	2	3	4	5	6	7	8	9	10	11	12	13	14	15	16
17	18	19	20	21	22	23	24	25	26	27	28	29	30	31	32
33	34	35	36	37	38	39	40	41	42	43	44	45	46	47	48
49	50	51	52	53	54	55	56	57	58	59	60	61	62	63	64
65	66	67	68	69	70	71	72	73	74	75	76	77	78	79	80
81	82	83	84	85	86	87	88	89	90	91	92	93	94	95	96

The most straightforward arrangement is to have alternate spreads distributing the colour evenly throughout the book. Printing CMYK on one side of each section, followed by a one-colour pass on the reverse, results in full colour appearing every alternate spread. This would print on three sheets, with 32 pages to a sheet.

Another configuration would be to 'bunch' the colour section front and back

1	2	3	4	5	6	7	8	9	10	11	12	13	14	15	16
17	18	19	20	21	22	23	24	25	26	27	28	29	30	31	32
33	34	35	36	37	38	39	40	41	42	43	44	45	46	47	48
49	50	51	52	53	54	55	56	57	58	59	60	61	62	63	64
65	66	67	68	69	70	71	72	73	74	75	76	77	78	79	80
81	82	83	84	85	86	87	88	89	90	91	92	93	94	95	96

By running a colour block of 16 pages at the front and the back of the book these areas would carry all the colour. In this example, pages 1–16 and 81–96 would be printed together and then cut. The 16-page solid colour section can print anywhere as long as it matches another 16-page section allowing 32 pages to print together.

Additionally you may want to add a two-colour section as well

1	2	3	4	5	6	7	8	9	10	11	12	13	14	15	16
17	18	19	20	21	22	23	24	25	26	27	28	29	30	31	32
33	34	35	36	37	38	39	40	41	42	43	44	45	46	47	48
49	50	51	52	53	54	55	56	57	58	59	60	61	62	63	64
65	66	67	68	69	70	71	72	73	74	75	76	77	78	79	80
81	82	83	84	85	86	87	88	89	90	91	92	93	94	95	96

16 pages with two colours can be added in matching sections. In this instance, the two-colour section, appears in the second and fourth signatures.

Signature

A signature or section is a sheet of paper folded to form several pages. Signatures of a book are then gathered and bound. In a section-sewn book, the sections are sewn after gathering. The term signature refers to a letter at the tail of each section, running in alphabetical order, that acts as a guide to the gatherer.

Alternatively…

1	2	3	4	5	6	7	8	9	10	11	12	13	14	15	16
17	18	19	20	21	22	23	24	25	26	27	28	29	30	31	32
33	34	35	36	37	38	39	40	41	42	43	44	45	46	47	48
49	50	51	52	53	54	55	56	57	58	59	60	61	62	63	64
65	66	67	68	69	70	71	72	73	74	75	76	77	78	79	80
81	82	83	84	85	86	87	88	89	90	91	92	93	94	95	96

Making the front of the book colour heavy, signatures one and three, two and five, and four and six would print together, again as matching pairs.

Adding a special colour

1	2	3	4	5	6	7	8	9	10	11	12	13	14	15	16
17	18	19	20	21	22	23	24	25	26	27	28	29	30	31	32
33	34	35	36	37	38	39	40	41	42	43	44	45	46	47	48
49	50	51	52	53	54	55	56	57	58	59	60	61	62	63	64
65	66	67	68	69	70	71	72	73	74	75	76	77	78	79	80
81	82	83	84	85	86	87	88	89	90	91	92	93	94	95	96

Here a special colour has been added to the fourth and sixth signature.

Again, as long as there are matching pairs, the colour fall can be moved

1	2	3	4	5	6	7	8	9	10	11	12	13	14	15	16
17	18	19	20	21	22	23	24	25	26	27	28	29	30	31	32
33	34	35	36	37	38	39	40	41	42	43	44	45	46	47	48
49	50	51	52	53	54	55	56	57	58	59	60	61	62	63	64
65	66	67	68	69	70	71	72	73	74	75	76	77	78	79	80
81	82	83	84	85	86	87	88	89	90	91	92	93	94	95	96

16 two-colour pages can be added in matching sections. Now the special colour falls in the second and fifth signatures.

Client: Spine Publishing
Design: Rose Design
Process: Book with
uncoated and silk stocks,
printed single colour
throughout and
perfect bound

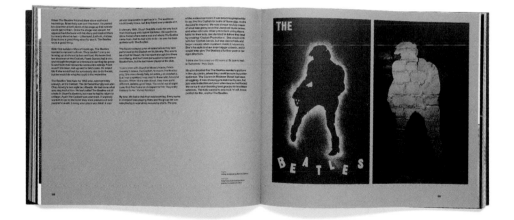

The Beatles – The True Beginnings

For a book about The Beatles, Rose Design divided two distinct types of information by using different stocks. A brown-coloured uncoated stock carries archival photography and the main text sections. A plain silk stock carries a series of large quotes and non-archival photography by Sandro Sodano. The two stocks enhance the contrast between the high quality of Sodano's recent studio photography and the mixed quality of the archival images.

The book is formed of 14 eight-page, four-colour sections on silk stock; and 11 eight-page, two-colour sections on uncoated stock that are printed and spliced to create the mixed pagination.

Rankin Works

Various different methods for book binding exist including perfect, lay-flat and edition. This design by Form for Booth-Clibborn Editions' publication *Rankin Works* uses edition binding, a method that gives the product a long life and allows the pages to lay flat when the book is opened.

Hardback publications like this usually have a dust-jacket. Originally they offered protection against dirt and dust as the name suggests, but more recently they have become an integral graphic extension of the book and a key device for promotion.

Client: Rankin

Design: Form Design

Process: Four-colour, edition-bound book

RankinWorks

Edition binding

Case or edition binding is a common hard cover book-binding method where the signatures are sewn together, the spine is flattened, endsheets are applied and a cloth strip is added to the spine. Then the hard covers are attached. The spine is usually rounded and grooves are made along the cover edge to act as hinges.

Headband / Tailband

A headband or tailband is a piece of cloth tape that covers the top or bottom of the spine. It is both decorative and provides protection to the spine.

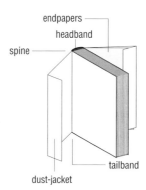

endpapers

headband

spine

tailband

dust-jacket

Format Edition binding

The Clash

The Clash were an influential punk rock band that showed great endurance throughout its career. For *The Clash. Photographs* book project featuring images by Bob Gruen, Form gave the product extra durability by including a slipcase to store and protect it. The cover of the book is decorated with industrial warning chevrons alluding to the direct nature of the music The Clash played throughout their career. Once the book is opened, the chevrons provide a strong visual frame for the images that it contains.

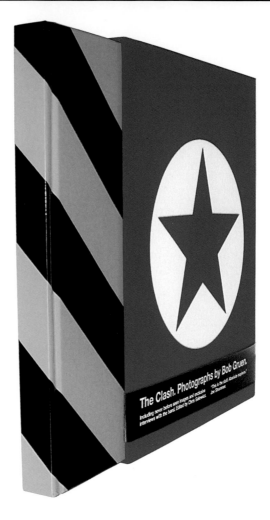

Slipcase

A slipcase is generally a box structure made from a hard and durable substrate to contain and protect a book, or group several books together in one package. In addition to protection, a slipcase adds another element to the presentation of the product. It is open at one end so that the book's spine is visible and will naturally have slightly bigger dimensions than the item(s) it is to contain, however it is not so big that the contents do not fit snugly inside.

Client: The Clash

Design: Form Design

Process: Four-colour edition-bound book in slipcase

In Feburary 1979 The Clash set off on their first American tour.

Caroline: Part of the punk ethic was to refuse to be in any way gracious to anyone from the record company who came backstage. My charm helped a bit, especially when we ran out of money halfway through the tour, and I had to go on my knees to the record company and ask for more cash to finish the tour. But they did it because The Clash were playing fantastic gigs that were absolute sell-outs.

You have to understand that The Clash never ever did a gig that wasn't rampacked. From the first gig they ever did in London. Because of the build-up, with everyone knowing there was something happening. Unlike the Pistols who for the first few gigs were building the punk audience. By the time The Clash came along there was already quite a big scene, so they never ever had to do a gig where they had to win over the audience. The audience was so ready and up for it. I don't think there's been any band in the history of rock'n'roll that has had that experience. Even the Beatles, the Rolling Stones had to build an audience. But the audience was there for The Clash, ready for it.

Bob: The Clash liked America in general. Coming from England, the whole country seems like Disneyland. That's what America does well: we are big and bright and candy-coloured and pink and yellow and "red, white and blue". You come to America and it's fast food and fast girls and fast cars and big, wide-open streets. In America anyone says anything to anybody - pretty loudly. The band really liked that swaggering American attitude and the big cars.

Client: Canongate Books Ltd.
Design: Pentagram
(Angus Hyland)
Process: Paperback perfect-bound series in slipcase

Canongate Pocket Canons

Here is an example of a slipcase used for packaging several books together as one product. This project for Canongate Books Ltd. was for 12 extracts from the King James Bible in pocket form. Pentagram partner, Angus Hyland, approached the project as though he were designing covers for modern fiction, but used tonally dark stock photography to reflect the seriousness of the content and to avoid a particular photographer's style.

The results include an image of a nuclear explosion for *Revelation*, a modern equivalent of Armageddon, and a Kafkaesque silhouette for the book of *Job*. Packaged as Old Testament and New Testament, each group of six volumes is contained in a slipcase. Each volume has an introduction written by a figure from contemporary culture.

Client: Boym & Partners /
Princeton Architectural Press
Design: Karlssonwilker Inc.
Process: Four-colour litho
brochure with die-cut 'handle'

Boym & Partners Book

In its design for a book about industrial design studio Boym & Partners for Princeton Architectural Press, Karlssonwilker Inc. killed two birds with one stone by putting a die-cut hole in the front cover. In addition to providing a glimpse inside the book, the removed cover stock was used as the book launch party invite/drinks coaster. The design also includes an innovative carry handle hidden between the centre pages.

Die cut

A die cut is a process that uses a steel die to cut away a section of a page. It is mainly used for decorative purposes to enhance the visual performance of a design rather than serving a physical function.

Die cuts have many uses from creating pieces with unusual shapes to creating apertures that allow the user to see inside a publication, as some of the examples provided show, including the cover of this publication.

Die cuts produce a range of effects from the striking to the subtle. The front cover of this book has a die cut revealing the colour of the first page of the text block. More subtle applications include rounded die-cut corners, making printed matter physically 'softer', see pages 80–81.

Client: Violet Editions
Design: Aboud Sodano
Process: Four-colour book with tip-ins cut to different sizes in polystyrene case with magnifying glass, loose-leaf posters and inserts

You Can Find Inspiration in Everything*

This book for clothing designer Paul Smith designed by Aboud Sodano is quite an interesting package. It came in a polystyrene case with a magnifying glass and a pattern for a suit jacket that has multiple arms.

*And if You Can't, Look Again

The book itself has several tip-ins and multiple covers (as shown). The main picture shows the introduction page that has been cut to a different height than the regular pages and is written in multiple languages. The theme of the publication is discovery and excitement, and this is certainly portrayed through the various format choices made.

paul smith: a most benevolent marve

paul smith: en wunder im besten sinne

paul smith: un prodigo estremamente benevolo

paul smith: une pure merveille

william g

william gibson

william gibson

ウィリアム・

ポール・スミス

reader:
go forwards,
don't go backwards,
and remember,
many a true string
said in vest.

Client: Levi's
Design: The Kitchen
Process: Ten die-cut card pages contained in clam-shell box

Levi's RED Press Pack (above)
Each fashion season throws up different themes that need to be worked into the designs that promote the clothing. The theme for this press brochure for Levi's RED was glass. The Kitchen used die-cut pages to reduce the photography of Tim Bret-Day to shards creating an unusual piece that is in harmony with the season's theme.

CMYK RGB (right)
SAS created this publication to showcase its work and promote its design practice. A thin plastic fluorescent bookmark is cover mounted on the book and detailed with various figures and statistics that illustrate the everyday working reality of the studio, such as 11.5 years, 1,144 late night pizzas, 5 toasters, 2 microwaves culminating in 1 SAS. The book is printed with a black fore edge (with black top, bottom and fore edges, that is), achieved by bleed printing.

Bleed printing
When the printed information extends past where the page will be trimmed so that the colours or images continue to the edge of the cut page.

Client: SAS
Design: SAS
Process: 280-page company brochure bleed printed with solid black top, bottom and fore edges

Client: Tank
Design: Tank
Process: Miniature special edition magazine

ANTONIO BERARDI

365 days later

TANK

Some of the most impressive design in the 20th century centred on magazine design, a field that continues to innovate. Similar choice factors exist as for book format decisions, although magazines are more disposable by nature.

Magazine designers tend to focus on the content rather than the physical format, sticking with a particular format for economic reasons and for certainty, as there is no point rethinking every aspect of the design with each issue too regularly, although some people do as the Tank example opposite illustrates. Standard paper sizes, particularly A4, dominate the shelves of newsagents although over the last decade paper stock selections have been upgraded as four-colour printing has become the norm.

Magazines are produced for everything from high fashion to industrial minerals, celebrity gossip to finance, and each end-use sector has different requirements and lifetimes. For example, the disposable nature of celebrity gossip means that the magazines that carry it use low quality stock because the content is 'throw-away'. Contrast this to an academic journal that will be retained and stored for years.

Tank – Big Fashion Issue (left)

For its 'big fashion' issue Tank magazine went miniature to create a pocket-sized edition. It was published in response to people asking when Tank was going to become a 'proper' magazine. Tank encouraged rumours that it was intending to publish a 'big fashion' special issue that people assumed would be in a large format size. The product's dimensions are 70mm x 55mm, with the back half of the magazine printed upside down to give two different magazines in one issue

Client: Tank

Design: Tank

Process: Various issues in different formats ranging from the 350mm x 280mm oversized to 70mm x 55mm miniature version

Tank

Generally, magazines stick to the same format because in such a competitive market having a product that is easy to recognise through being consistent from one issue to the next is considered a good thing. This is not the philosophy of *Tank* magazine. As these examples show, the magazine has used various formats ranging from a 350mm x 280mm oversized format to a 70mm x 55mm miniature version.

Changing the dimensions of the publication and the positioning of its title do not seem to have held back the commercial viability of *Tank* magazine. For its fifth anniversary issue, 20% of the print run, or one in five copies, was a special collectors' edition printed without any images.

Format Scale

Mind

In its design for *Mind* magazine Tank used a variety of formatting techniques. The publication is made from eight sheets of paper accordion-folded into 32-page sections and sewn into a book block. The book block is without a cover so that the stitching is exposed and becomes a feature rather than being hidden away as is usual.

The outer fold on each page is perforated allowing readers to tear pages open to reveal the complete pagination. The gradual tearing this process requires leaves the book increasingly ragged on the outer edge. Rather than feeling destroyed in any way though, the publication becomes more individual and personal to the reader.

Accordion fold

Two or more parallel folds that go in opposite directions and open out like an accordion. Also called concertina fold.

Client: Mind
Design: Tank
Process: 544-page
magazine, printed as
perforated accordion-fold
sections and left as
an open binding

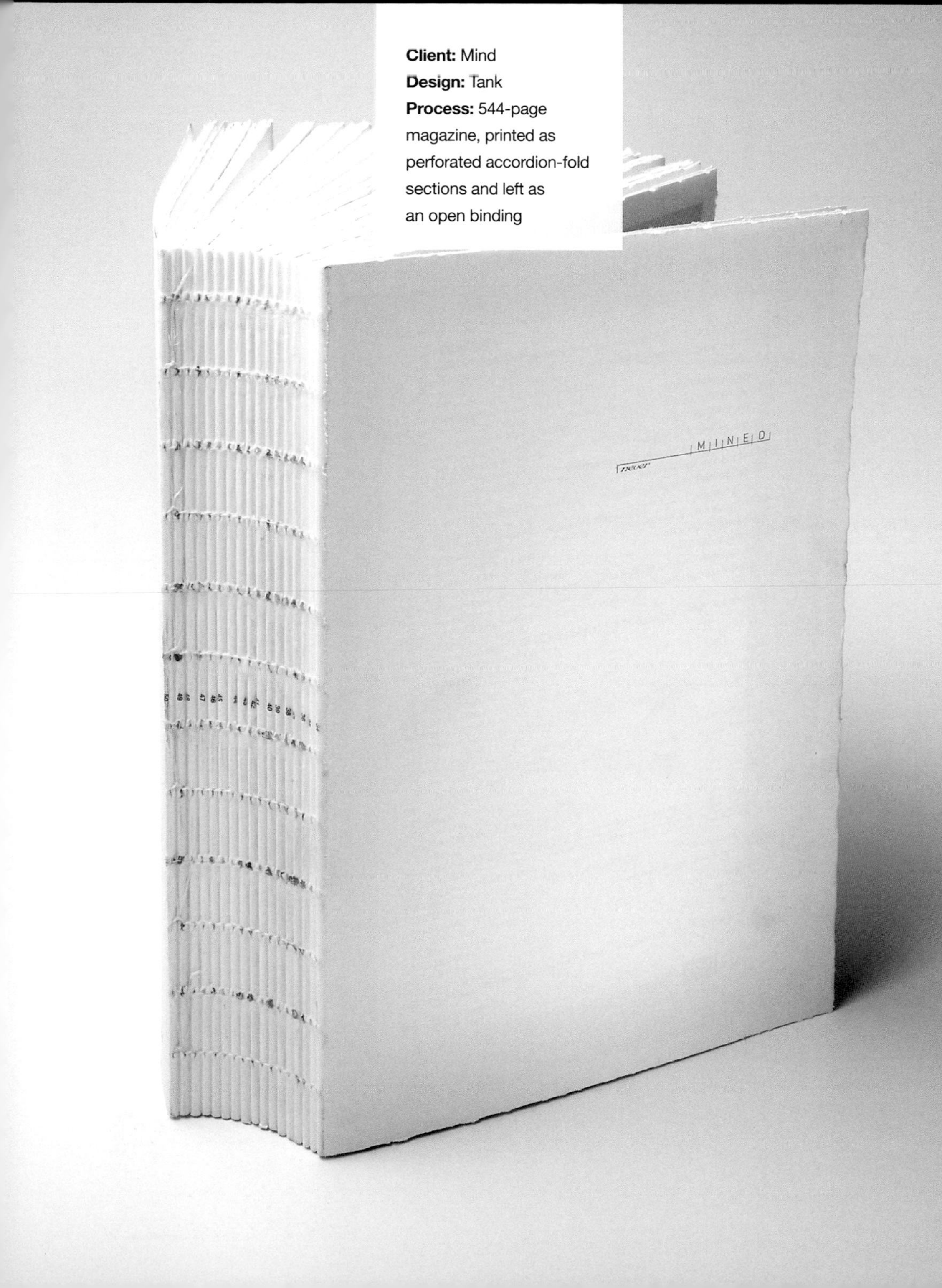

M I N E D

Client: Self-initiated
Design: FI@33
Process: Four-colour litho
oversized loose-leaf journal

Ampersand (right)

This design by Frost Design for a D&AD newsletter borrows heavily from newspapers in terms of its format, design and typography, which includes Jim-dashes (short rules dividing information), kickers (lines of copy appearing above or below an article), necklines (white spaces under running heads), standfirsts (introductory paragraphs), and mastheads (titles and visual keystones of a publication).

The use of this format lends the presented information a currency and authority that compels people to read it.

Trans-form
> Magazine (left)

For a publication containing images of cranes on the skyline, Fl@33 chose a loose-leaf oversized magazine format. The format selection marries with the oversized scale of the machinery depicted in the photographs.

Client: D&AD
Design: Frost Design
Process: Single-colour print on newsprint

PREMIERE ISSUE, BI-ANNUAL AUTUMN/WINTER 2001 UK£ 4.99

ANOTHER GAZINE

FOR MEN AND WOMEN

Client: Another Magazine

Design: Art direction by Stella McCartney

Process: Four-panel gatefold printed in four colours, tipped-in to perfect binding

Gatefold

A gatefold has extra panels that fold into the central spine of the publication with parallel folds so that they meet in the middle of the page. The extended pages are folded and cut shorter than the standard publication pages so that they can nest correctly. Gatefolds are commonly used in magazines for pull-out posters or in books for large-scale illustrations, photographs or graphics.

Throw

The throw is a sheet of paper that is folded into a publication, typically with larger dimensions than the work that contains it, and possibly of a different stock. It can be used to showcase a particular image, example or other visual element by allowing a larger scale to be used, and better printability if a better stock is used. This gatefold contains a throw for *Another Magazine* that was art directed by Stella McCartney.

Chris Robinson, lead singer of The Black Crowes, has just
completed a world tour promoting his latest album, Lions.

CONCEPT AND ART DIRECTION STELLA McCARTNEY
PHOTOGRAPHY MATTHIAS VRIENS AT WALTER SCHUPFER
MAKE-UP FERIDE USLU AT FRAME
HAIR ROLANDO BEAUCHAMP FOR BUMBLE & BUMBLE
MANICURIST BERNADETTE THOMPSON AT ZANE AGENCY
PHOTOGRAPHIC ASSISTANTS JASON HILLS, SAM BIFFA
AND PETER BURGSTALLER
MAKE UP ASSISTANT MEZO
RETOUCHING RAPHAEL DANAN AT 4TH-FLOOR NY
PRODUCTION TERESA FARRELL AT WALTER SCHUPFER
PROCESSING SMALL DARK ROOM
THANKS TO MILK STUDIOS NY

BLACK & WHITE:
A Hollywood Classic

Stella McCartney stepped out of the design studio to guest
art direct the centrefold exclusively for this issue of Another
Magazine. Featuring her friends, actress Kate Hudson and
husband, musician Chris Robinson, Stella McCartney has
created the ultimate pin-up statement. Her vision of male and
female sexuality for this season is romantic, not too revealing
and ultimately sexy. She shows that friendships and a loving
relationship are the strongest link. Stella McCartney will
be showing her debut collection under her own name this
season, during Paris Fashion Week.

Oscar nominated actress Kate Hudson is set to appear in two
forthcoming films this year: Four Feathers by Shekhar Kapur,
the director of Elizabeth, and How To Loose A Guy In 10
Days by Mike Newell.
106 ANOTHER MAGAZINE

Another Magazine

This example of a gatefold for *Another Magazine* is a four-panel, double-sided fold out. It features Chris Robinson from the rock group The Black Crowes below and actress Kate Hudson above, with art direction by Stella McCartney.

The three panels that open out are folded and cut narrower than the standard pages in the publication so that they can nest inside it. A gatefold needs to be tipped-in to the publication that contains it.

Client: Creative Review

Design: Pentagram
(Angus Hyland)

Process: Four-colour litho
with perforations

The Poster

Posters surround us though we are not always conscious that they are there. On billboards, buses and taxis posters are endemic throughout the urban environment. However, not all posters are pasted on to walls as some of the examples featured in this section. We encounter posters in situations that may sometimes be surprising.

Posters must catch our attention in a short space of time; this can be achieved in many ways, though principally through visual devices. However, posters are sometimes designed for specific hand-held products giving a designer more leeway to work with format aspects such as stock, size and dimensions.

A poster that is part of a hand-held product may be used as a means to organise information, provide a larger format with which to display an image, or serve other purposes.

Tear Me Up (left)

This poster for *Creative Review* magazine designed by Angus Hyland at Pentagram was to promote a student subscription offer. It invited students, and others for that matter, to deconstruct the poster and create something new.

The poster is a double sheet, with a fold along the top edge separating the top TEAR ME UP from the bottom sheet. Each letter is perforated through the middle providing an element of interaction so that as they are removed, details of the subscription are revealed.

Showthrough

Client: Alexander McQueen
Design: Mono Design
Process: A2 poster printed
four-colour backed with
40gsm bible paper, folded to
A5 for mailing

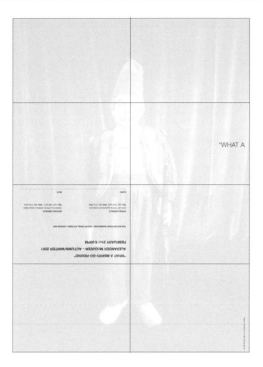

Alexander McQueen Invitation

Most posters are for sticking up on walls. The McQueen poster by Mono Design was, however, an invitation to an event. As it had to be mailed, it was folded to A5.

On one of these panels on the reverse side of the design, details of the invitation and event were printed. Bible paper, one of the thinnest papers, was deliberately chosen to allow a high degree of showthrough to occur.

A series paper sizes

4A0	1680mm x 2376mm
2A0	1188mm x 1680mm
A0	840mm x 1188mm
A1	594mm x 840mm
A2	420mm x 594mm
A3	297mm x 420mm
A4	210mm x 297mm
A5	148.5mm x 210mm
A6	105mm x 148.5mm
A7	74mm x 105mm
A8	52.5mm x 74mm
A9	37mm x 52.5mm
A10	26.25mm x 37mm

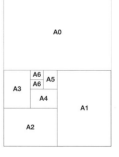

Showthrough

Showthrough or strikethrough is where printing inks can be seen on the reverse side of the page. Particularly common with thin paper stocks and/or those with low loadings of fillers and coating, it is generally considered undesirable but, as this example shows, can be used creatively.

Ravensbourne Prospectus

Rather than create a publication with a spine for the 2002/2003 prospectus for Ravensbourne College of Design and Communication, MadeThought created a folded poster that opens to reveal a student hard at work. This is in stark contrast to the majority of prospectuses that normally have a similar format to this book. This format also allows the information to be arranged according to the folded panels, bringing a hierarchical order to the piece.

Client: Ravensbourne College
Design: MadeThought
Process: Four-colour fold-down poster/prospectus

Spot varnish

Spot varnishing is the application of varnish to a specific area of a printed piece, usually full coverage of an image.

In-line or 'wet' varnishing as a fifth or sixth colour during printing adds a wet layer of varnish on a wet layer of ink. As they dry they absorb into the stock together which diminishes the impact. Off-line varnishing applies the varnish as a separate pass once the inks have dried and results in extra glossiness as less is absorbed by the stock.

A UV spot varnish is a high-gloss varnish applied to selected areas to enhance impact or form part of the graphic design. A raised texture can be achieved using UV spot varnish.

Client: Haworth
Design: North
Process: Four-colour brochure, gatefold back cover, several throws, spot varnish, poster wrap

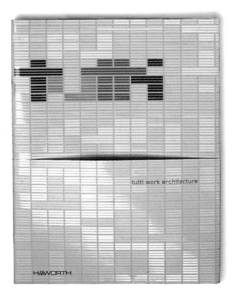

Tutti

This design for *Tutti Work Architecture* by North is a poster-wrapped publication that contains a number of throws and a three-panel gatefold back cover (pictured).

The brochure explores the way that changing the work environment can alter and foster a more productive working culture in an organisation.

The bar design appears throughout the publication, sometimes as a graphic and sometimes as a more subtle spot varnish.

Format Spot varnish

Large poster sizes

Larger-scale poster work is expressed in sheet size, for example 16-, 32-, 48-, 64- or 96-sheet. The individual sections used to construct these large posters are known as 4-sheet, being the size of four sheets of double crown.

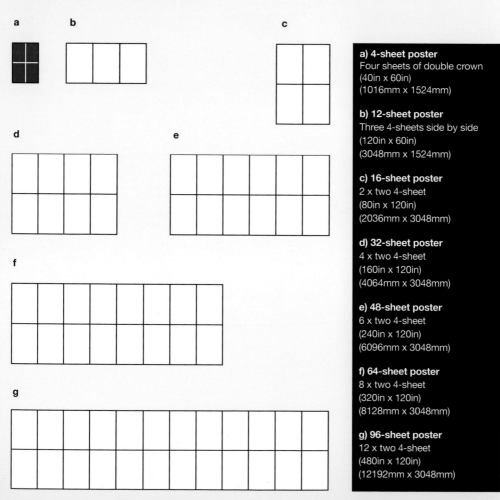

a) 4-sheet poster
Four sheets of double crown
(40in x 60in)
(1016mm x 1524mm)

b) 12-sheet poster
Three 4-sheets side by side
(120in x 60in)
(3048mm x 1524mm)

c) 16-sheet poster
2 x two 4-sheet
(80in x 120in)
(2036mm x 3048mm)

d) 32-sheet poster
4 x two 4-sheet
(160in x 120in)
(4064mm x 3048mm)

e) 48-sheet poster
6 x two 4-sheet
(240in x 120in)
(6096mm x 3048mm)

f) 64-sheet poster
8 x two 4-sheet
(320in x 120in)
(8128mm x 3048mm)

g) 96-sheet poster
12 x two 4-sheet
(480in x 120in)
(12192mm x 3048mm)

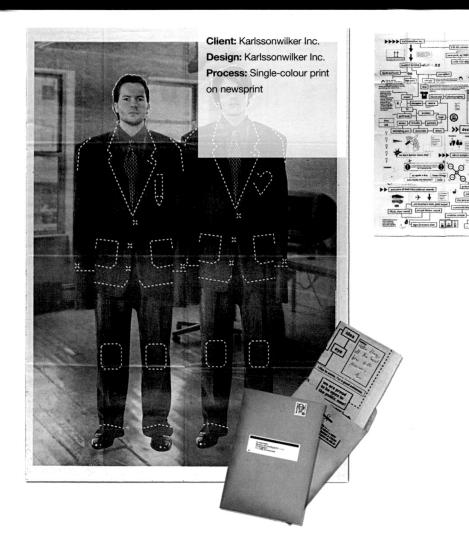

Client: Karlssonwilker Inc.

Design: Karlssonwilker Inc.

Process: Single-colour print on newsprint

Karlssonwilker Inc. Opening Invite (above)

Karlssonwilker Inc. designed this card to announce the opening of its design studio. It is a poster (22.5in x 31.5in or 571mm x 800mm) on newsprint with three parallel folds and a cross fold to reduce it to 1/16 size to enable it to fit into envelopes for mailing.

Small poster sizes

International standards govern paper sizes and also apply to poster formats such as these Deutsche Industrie Norm (DIN) standard sizes: A0 841mm x 1189mm, B0 1000mm x 1414mm, A1 594mm x 841mm, B1 707mm x 1000mm.

Format Large poster sizes

Client: Making Space Publishers
Design: SAS
Process: 21 A2 posters contained in polypropylene silk-screened bag

Inside Cover

This catalogue designed by SAS for 'Inside Cover' exhibition challenges the preconceptions of the traditional brochure form. Rather than bind the pages into a coherent whole they are instead collated into a bag that closes with press studs. The titles of the posters are printed on the outside fold edge so that when they are stacked they can be identified. Each poster features an exhibit from the different designers and artists. Opposite 'The Bookmaker' by Deb Rindl can be seen top left and 'Hunting' by Henk Hans Hilvering, top right. Below is 'Office Orchestra' by Andrea Chappell and Cherry Goddard that features all the office equipment that can be 'played', with an original score by Nick Lee.

Client: Liberty
Design: SEA Design
Process: Etched acrylic

The Object

The wide nature of possible printed objects means that some of the more interesting and innovative print design can be found here in this section. Less confined by established norms than books, magazines and posters give designers licence to let the creative juices flow to produce one-off pieces using the full arsenal of design aspects.

Mailers, menus, flyers or invites all have potential for creative folding and finishing, die cutting, stock or substrate selection, as the example opposite shows. One can even go into the third dimension with pop-ups.

While it is possible to use all the design tools on such pieces it may not always be appropriate to do so. The expectations of the client and the most effective way to communicate with the target audience should take precedence over frivolity. That said, as our examples show, it is possible to satisfy a brief with some wonderful and exciting designs.

Liberty (left)
SEA Design made an imaginative substrate choice for these invites for Matthew Williamson's 'Lifestyle' show at Liberty in London. Using acrylic of different colours, the simple informative design is etched into the substrate. The format size also makes the invite suitable to use as a coaster.

Client: Woven
Design: MadeThought
Process: Four colour
and spot varnish in box with
printed inners with block
colour and spot varnish overlay

Woven

Woven is the trend-forecast book for the fashion and textile industry. The Autumn/Winter 2003/2004 edition is a loose-leaf binder contained in a cloth-covered box, the inside of which is printed with the face of the model that appears throughout the pages of the book.

Format Containers

Client: Design For Freedom
Design: Build
Process: Transfer on to product

Design For Freedom

Substrates do not have to be paper-based or two dimensional as this mug designed by Mike Place at Build illustrates. Printing on mugs and other items is commonplace for promotional items and is a reminder that virtually anything can be used as a substrate for a design.

Build specialises in design for print and this mug designed for Design For Freedom's Mug Shop project marks a departure from the usual media that its work appears on.

The Mug Shop project aims to produce and deliver limited edition designer coffee mugs by a group of selected artists.

Transfer or decal

This is a design on a substrate that is intended to be transferred to the surface of another substrate, usually glass, wood, metal or ceramic.

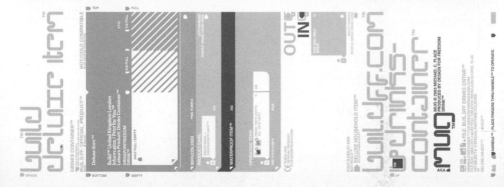

Format The Object

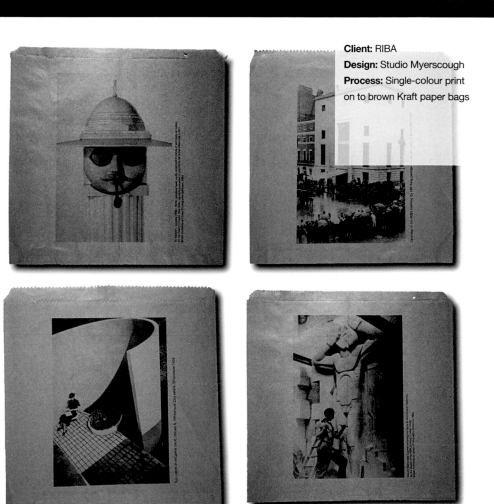

Client: RIBA
Design: Studio Myerscough
Process: Single-colour print
on to brown Kraft paper bags

RIBA Bookshops

Bags are everywhere: disposable printed matter that we receive every time we buy something. Studio Myerscough took disposability to the hilt in its design for the Royal Institute of British Architecture (RIBA) bookshop bags by using an off-the-shelf form as a substrate; brown paper grocery bags. The bags are printed with an ongoing series of images from the RIBA archive and so juxtapose the disposable with the permanent.

Brown Kraft paper bags

Most paper bags are made from Kraft paper, a coarse paper made from wood pulp and noted for its strength. In unbleached grades, it is primarily used as packaging material and as it is not made specifically to reproduce a consistent image, it has slight colour variations that affect any images printed on this stock.

Different types of folds

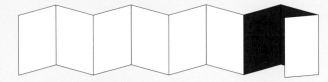

Front / back accordion fold With three parallel folds, the two-panel outer wings fold into and out of the centre. The double panel centre serves as the cover.

Mock book fold Essentially an accordion fold where the penultimate two panels form a cover that the other panels fold into to create a book.

 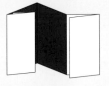

Front / back gatefold An extra double panel that folds inside the front and/or back panel

Triple parallel fold Parallel folds that create a section that nests within the cover panels, with a front opening. May be used with maps.

Format The Object

Back / front folder Wings either side of the central panel have a double parallel fold so that they can fold around and cover both sides of the central panel.

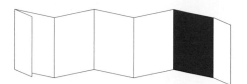

Half cover from behind An accordion fold where the penultimate panel forms a back cover that the other panels fold into to create a book, but the half-size end panel folds around the book from behind to cover the front together with the half-size first panel.

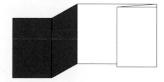

Duelling z-fold Z-fold wings fold into the centre panel and meet in the middle.

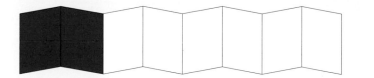

Harmonica self-cover folder An accordion fold where the first two panels form a cover that the other panels fold into. The first two panels need to be larger than the others to allow for creep.

Double gatefold The gatefold has three panels that fold in towards the centre of the publication.

Frost Design Portfolio

With so many publications and documents in the A4 format, something rather different and more dramatic can be achieved with folding techniques. Folding adds to the physical texture of a piece and provides a novel way of dividing space or organising the elements in the design, in effect creating a physical grid to guide the design, as this example by Frost Design shows.

Concertina fold

Each fold runs opposite to the previous one to obtain a pleated result. The outer page needs to be larger than the inner pages to hide the rough folding edges of the final piece. Alternatively, a concertina can be folded in on itself, in which case the pages can be made incrementally smaller. The weight and type of paper have a bearing on this measurement.

Client: Frost Design
Design: Frost Design
Process: Concertina
litho print, bonded to outer
board with foil-blocked type

Minutes

Struktur used a concertina fold to produce a self-promotional calendar that is almost three metres long when unfolded. An obvious benefit here is that the folding method allows the size of the product to be condensed into a more manageable form, and also physically provides pages upon which to position the design. The overall length meant that it had to be printed in three sections that were then fixed together, heavy embossed greyboard ends were then glued on providing a protective carrier.

Client: Struktur
Design: Struktur
Process: 18-panel concertina fold, printed in three sections and bonded to greyboard cover

Format The Object

Client: FunLab
Design: KesselsKramer
Process: 12-panel concertina, bonded to outer die-cut wrap-cover

The Suitcase (above)

For 'The Suitcase' project for client FunLab at the Eindoven Design Academy in the Netherlands, KesselsKramer created a brochure with a concertina fold that emulates a suitcase in that the contents spill out when it is opened. The end page is die cut so that it can be wrapped around the folded brochure to close it.

The brochure documents the results of the project in which students were given a suitcase and constructed a personality for a fictional character using the possessions in the case as a vehicle.

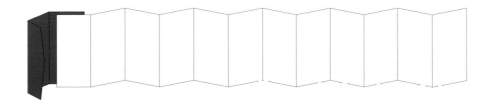

Format Concertina

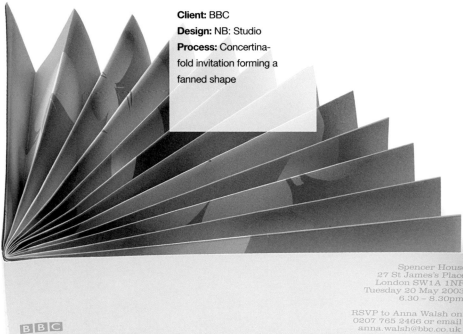

Client: BBC
Design: NB: Studio
Process: Concertina-fold invitation forming a fanned shape

Spencer House
27 St James's Place
London SW1A 1NR
Tuesday 20 May 2003,
6.30 – 8.30pm

RSVP to Anna Walsh on
0207 765 2466 or email
anna.walsh@bbc.co.uk

BBC

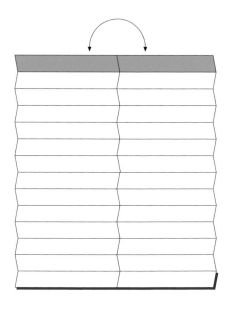

BBC Radio & Music Summer Reception Invite

This piece by NB: Studio for an invite for a 'BBC Radio & Music Summer Reception' perfectly illustrates the accordion fold, which is also known as a fan fold. The invite is made from a single sheet of paper with accordion or concertina folds along its length and then one right-angle fold to create a fan. A printed white substrate was then glued on to the outside. A combination of valley and mountain folds ensures that the fan retains its shape. The circular illusion of the fan is created by gluing the top two panels together.

Client: Tate Britain
Design: SEA Design
Process: Concertina-fold
information updaters

Tate Britain

SEA Design chose to use a concertina fold in its design for a literature system for the Tate galleries. A concertina fold is a folding method where each fold runs opposite to the previous one to obtain a pleated result. The fold physically divides up the area of the leaflet into equal manageable 'panels' on which the design can be organised.

Valley and Mountain folds
A valley fold is when you fold the paper towards yourself and for a mountain fold you fold it behind or away from yourself.

Adding value

Shown are the 17 print techniques used by Radley Yelder, many of which are discussed elsewhere in this publication. They range from a simple emboss and deboss, to special colours, die stamp, die cut, and others. Many of these techniques add texture to the page: an off-line varnish creates a subtle raised surface, while thermography (a process of fusing powder to printed areas) creates immediate impact.

Metallic
See page 24

Varnish
See front cover

Deboss

Thermography

Black and grey duotone

Letterpress

Embossing

Silver die stamp

Blind emboss

Matt varnish

Die cut
See front cover

Metallic halftone

Varnish with colour

Specials
See page 24

Four colour process
Prints CMYK

Halftone on special

Embossed mirror board

Client: Printed Stationery
Design: Radley Yeldar
Process: 17 postcards featuring a variety of print techniques, slipcase folder, single colour bellyband

Printed Stationery

Printed Stationery is a niche market stationery printing company that emphasises the importance of craftsmanship in its work. Radley Yeldar was able to use Printed Stationery's abilities in the production of its design. The product is a pack of 17 postcards produced as an accordion-folded strip, each one with a found image of a letter that together spell out Printed Stationery. Each letter is also produced with a specific printing or print finishing technique. For example the 'R' of Rolls Royce is printed with a varnish. Other techniques used include thermography, duotone, embossing, letterpress, die stamping, metallic halftone and mirror board.

Client: Photonica
Design: Frost Design
Process: Concertina
perforated 'stamps' with
perforated type forming
the logotype

Photonica Mailer

The versatility of the mailer can be seen in this example by Frost Design for the Photonica photo library that caters for the physical size and weight constraints inherent in it being an item for mailing, yet sacrifices nothing in terms of creativity or communication.

A small selection of the images from the photo library are displayed in the piece courtesy of a concertina fold pull-out. This folded section is bonded into a card wrap folder that is a more convenient size for sending through the postal system.

The four-colour design is perforated, like a sheet of stamps, allowing the images to be separated and used like swatches – providing an indication of the usage and variety of the full library of images.

Perforation
A series of cuts or holes manufactured on a form to weaken it for tearing. Press perforation or machine perforation refers to how the perforation is made, while blade perforation and wheel perforation refers to the cutting device used.

Format Perforation

Client: Beaux Arts
Design: Studio AS
Process: Four-colour litho with die-cut cover printed in silver

David Spiller Catalogue (above and below)
For a collection of David Spiller paintings that all featured circles, Studio AS used a die cut to hint at what lies within the catalogue's pages rather than an image.

The Rolling Stones (right)
This cover for The Rolling Stones' 'Bridges to Babylon' CD designed by Stefan Sagmeister and Hjalti Karlsson featured an illustration of an Assyrian lion by Kevin Murphy. The illustration is emphasised by a special filigree slipcase that outlines the lion with an intricate arabesque detail.

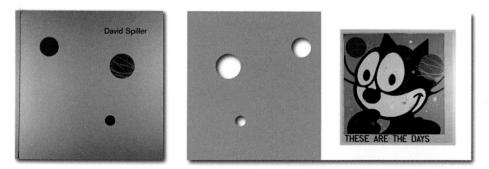

Die cut
A die cut is a shape that is cut into a substrate by using a specially shaped steel die.

Client: Rolling Stones
Design: Sagmeister Inc.
Process: Filigree slipcase
CD packaging

Filigree
Filigree is traditionally ornamental work in which fine gold or silver wire is used to create intricate patterns.

Format Die cut

Client: Lisa Pritchard Agency
Design: SEA Design
Process: Four-colour litho with die-cut corners

Lisa Pritchard Agency (above)
In this range of stationery for the Lisa Pritchard Agency in London, SEA Design produced a simple design dominated by the large scale of the typography. The roundness of the typographic characters is mirrored by the die-cut corners.

Design & Art Direction Mailers (right)
NB: Studio borrowed heavily on nostalgia in its design detailing the speakers for D&AD's annual event, with a design based on Top Trumps game cards. Speaker 'stats' are laid out in typical game card style and the cards have die-cut rounded corners. With a reply card for booking tickets, the size of the cards is also convenient for mailing. The cards came with a pack of stickers that were kiss cut.

Kiss cut
The stickers that came with these cards opposite were produced using a kiss cut. This is a method of die cutting whereby the face material of a self-adhesive substrate is die cut but not right through to the backing sheet. This enables the face material to be easily removed from the backing sheet.

Client: D&AD
Design: NB: Studio
Process: Four-colour litho on to pulp stock with kiss-cut sticker pack

Client: Design Museum
Design: Studio Myerscough
Process: Die-cut invitation
printed with graduating colour

RSVP on 020 7940 8783
or membership@designmus...
www.designmuseum.org

Somewhere Totally Else

For this 'Somewhere Totally Else' invite for the Design Museum in London,
Studio Myerscough created a piece printed with a graduating colour and a top
layer with die-cut type. As the counters in the letters (the space encircled by certain
characters such as 'R') fall out, incomplete letters are formed, creating a strong,
distinctive, typographic style.

Client: Recreation
Design: Form Design
Process: Die-cut invites
and 'Eames' stacking cards

Recreation

For the Recreation
identity for *Dazed &
Confused*/Topshop,
Form Design made an
object to embody the
characteristics of the
Recreation logo they
designed. Recreation
suggests rebirth or
reuse in another form.
Form turned the logo
into building bricks
that slot together,
enabling the recipient
to 'recreate' it as
something completely
different.

Client: Her House
Design: Studio Myerscough
Process: Litho-printed envelope invitations

Standard ISO C series envelope sizes

C0	917mm x 1297mm		C5	162mm x 229mm
C1	648mm x 917mm		C6	114mm x 162mm
C2	458mm x 648mm		C7	81mm x 114mm
C3	324mm x 458mm		DL	110mm x 220mm
C4	229mm x 324mm		C7/6	81mm x 162mm

Her House

Pictured are envelopes printed for an invite to an event at the studio owner's gallery/shop. An envelope, and certainly the back of an envelope, is a rarely used format on which to place design. By using standard (in this case DL) sized envelopes, the budget for the job can be invested in innovative design and printing rather than in the production of bespoke sized envelopes.

Format The Object

Client: Anne Klein
Design: Karlssonwilker Inc.
Process: Single-colour print
utilising showthrough

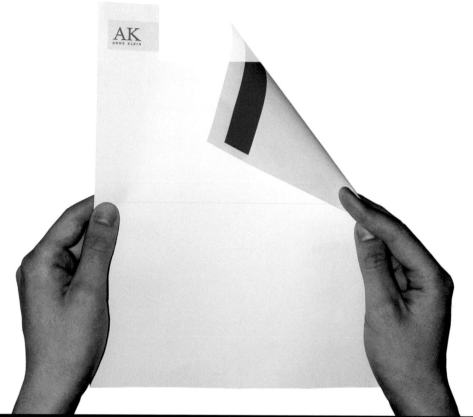

US paper standards

The ISO paper sizes are used throughout Europe and most of the rest of the world, not just in the UK. However, their usage is not common in the United States and Canada. The more commonly used standard American paper sizes are: Letter (216mm x 279mm) approximate to A4, Legal (216mm x 356mm) approximate to B4, Executive (184mm x 267mm) approximate to B5 and Ledger/Tabloid (279mm x 432mm) approximate to A3.

Anne Klein

Karlssonwilker Inc. designed a stationery system for all Anne Klein group affiliates including this letterhead. At first sight it appears to be a standard letterhead on American letter format paper. However, the logo on the letterhead is completed by the strikethrough of a subtle band of colour printed on the reverse.

Format Stationery

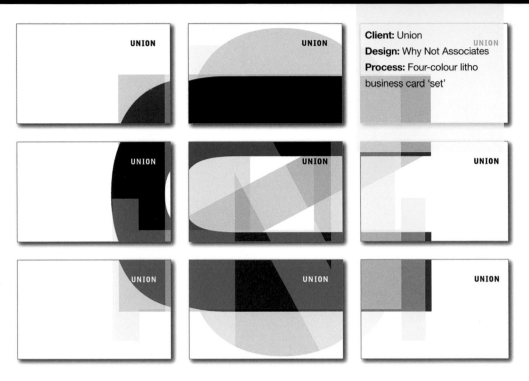

Client: Union
UNION
Design: Why Not Associates
Process: Four-colour litho
business card 'set'

Union

A business card is a pretty standard item you would think, but this design for Union by Why Not Associates extrapolates the format on which the logo is printed beyond that of the individual card. The logo, on the reverse of the cards, can only be seen in full when a block of nine cards are pieced together.

Standard stationery formats

The standard for business cards is the ID-1 format of 85.60mm x 53.98mm (3.370in x 2.125in). Another popular business card format is A8 (74mm x 52mm).

ISO paper sizes

A range of standard paper sizes exists to make life for designers and printers easier. The modern ISO (International Organisation for Standardisation) paper system is based on a width-to-height ratio of the square root of two (1:1.4142). Format A0 has an area of one square metre. The A series comprises a range of paper sizes that differ from the next size by a factor of 2 or ½. B series sizes are intermediate sizes and C series sizes are for envelopes that can contain A size stationery. RA and SRA are sheet sizes from which A sizes can be cut.

Client: Rabih Hage
Design: Hat-trick
Process: Die-cut stationery
range on uncoated stock

Rabih Hage

Hat-trick used the natural relationship between the letters 'r' and 'h' for stationery items for interior design company Rabih Hage. The 'r' is die cut out of the 'h' that is printed on all items to both represent the initials of Rabih Hage and provide a window to the interior of the items that is consistent with the business of the company, interiors. Shown above is a folded business card from the range.

Client: Profusion
Design: The Kitchen
Process: Laser-cut
stationery range

Profusion
Lindsay Green
60 Kingly Street SUK
London W1R 6D 973
T +44 (0) 20 7288 0
M +44 (0) 7752 500 3
lindsay.023@virgin.net

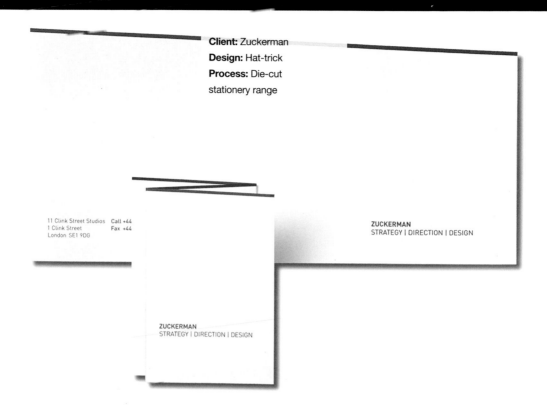

Client: Zuckerman
Design: Hat-trick
Process: Die-cut
stationery range

11 Clink Street Studios   Call +44
1 Clink Street   Fax +44
London SE1 9DG

ZUCKERMAN
STRATEGY | DIRECTION | DESIGN

ZUCKERMAN
STRATEGY | DIRECTION | DESIGN

Zuckerman (above)

The stationery package designed by Hat-trick design studio was tailored to client Zuckerman by using the initial 'Z' of Zuckerman. The format of each item was die cut on a bias to give a sloping top edge so that when folded – with a z-fold, naturally – the red stripe running along the top becomes a 'Z' as can be seen in the folded business card.

Profusion (left)

Creative destruction in design can produce both striking and effective results as this business card by The Kitchen for client Profusion illustrates. A laser was used to burn a pattern of holes into the substrate. On a white stock like this the laser creates small burn rings around each hole. These burn rings can be hidden by overprinting with a solid colour, but in this case creative director Rob Petrie intentionally left them visible. The burn marks appear on the back of the card as can be seen on the left of the photograph opposite.

Format Stationery

Client: MFI

Design: SAS

Process: Four-colour litho, saddle-stitched

MFI

Most company financial reports are presented in an A4 format publication and design agencies are encouraged to produce something original and attractive to pass positive associations on to the client company. When SAS designed a report for the half-year results of furniture company MFI it decided to only give the company half a report. The publication is A4 format in length but A6 in width (297mm x 105mm). The visual theme of the report is the idea that everything has been cut in half. On the cover, there's half a clock, a section of newspaper and a hand sneaking into frame, implying part of the brochure is missing. Inside the photography and typography follows a similar theme. Standard photographic portraits are cropped at the edge, and the charts and tables bleed off.

Client: Royal Mail
Design: HGVFelton
Process: Micro-printing

The Ad-dressing of Cats

You've read of several kinds of Cat,
And my opinion now is that
You should need no interpreter
To understand their character.
You now have learned enough to see
That Cats are much like you and me
And other people whom we find
Possessed of various types of mind.
For some are sane and some are mad
And some are good and some are bad
And some are better, some are worse—
But all may be described in verse.
You've seen them both at work and games,
And learnt about their proper names,
Their habits and their habitat:
But
How would you ad-dress a Cat?

Royal Mail

Perhaps the overriding consideration in creating designs for postage stamps is the very small size of the format. As most stamps convey images of people, places or things, this is manageable. Words are a different matter and require special techniques as this design by HGVFelton for the Royal Mail illustrates. The stamp was to celebrate English poet T. S. Eliot and his poem *The Ad-dressing of Cats*. Using micro-printing, the full text is reproduced on the stamp such that it is clearly legible, although you may need a magnifying glass to read it. This stamp is part of a series of six celebrating the centenary of the Nobel Prize.

Format Size

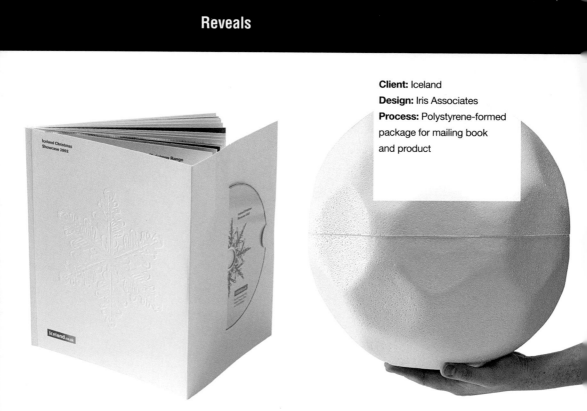

Client: Iceland
Design: Iris Associates
Process: Polystyrene-formed package for mailing book and product

Iceland Press Release (above and below)

Iris Associates created something extraordinary for food retailer Iceland's Christmas food range mailer to journalists. Not content with a brochure and showcase CD, the studio packaged it all in a snowball that received extensive coverage in both consumer and design media.

Lucian Freud Invite (right)

Die cuts are a simple yet highly effective mechanism for creating a dramatic and inventive design as this example by Radley Yeldar illustrates. The piece is an invite commissioned by UBS Investment Bank as part of a hospitality programme for Tate Britain. It is sterile except for the words 'Private view', but a centred die cut gives a private view of what is inside the invite, a painting by Lucian Freud entitled 'Head of a Naked Girl'.

Client: UBS Investment Bank
Design: Radley Yeldar
Process: Die-cut invitation

Private view

Client: National Portrait Gallery
Design: NB: Studio
Process: Five-colour
stand-up cards

National Portrait Gallery (above)

These invites created by NB: Studio for London's National Portrait Gallery for the 'Schweppes Photographic Portrait Prize 2003' are in the style of a photo frame complete with a hinged back foot. Each invite displays one of the competing images. The format borrows heavily from display cards produced for in-store promotions to allow the image to be presented in much the same way as an actual photo would be.

OXO (right)

For this cookbook for OXO, Tank focused on how such publications are used and created something more user-friendly than the traditional format. A magnetised metal substrate was chosen for the cover allowing the cookbook to be stuck to the fridge and the pages are laminated so that static electricity will hold them to each other so they do not flip over, and also enables them to be wiped clean. Another inspired touch is that each recipe has the ingredients printed on to a Post-it®-style note that can be detached when the reader goes to the supermarket.

Client: OXO
Design: Tank
Process: Wiro-bound, four-colour book with laminated pages and a metal cover stock

sausage cassoulet

Client: Melt London
Design: Agitprop
Process: Six-panel concertina fold, die cut and supported by two hardback boards sealed by a rubber band

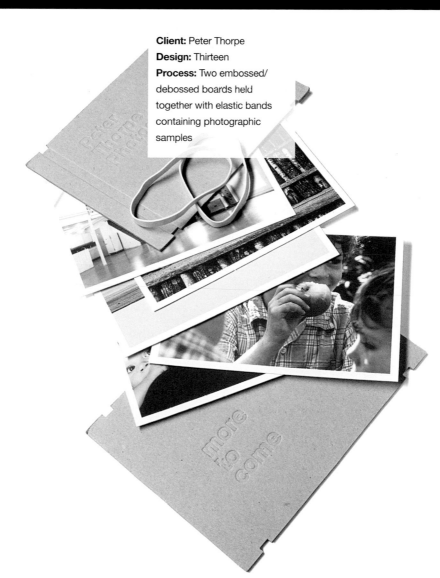

Client: Peter Thorpe
Design: Thirteen
Process: Two embossed/debossed boards held together with elastic bands containing photographic samples

Peter Thorpe Photography (above)

This mailer for Peter Thorpe Photography by Thirteen uses two elastic bands to hold together facing embossed boards. Flipping over the board with the address label reveals the photographer's name debossed into the substrate. The boards also protect the photographic samples that they contain.

Melt London (left)

Agitprop based this mailer for fashion label Melt London featuring images by Zed Nelson on a six-panel concertina fold. To convert it into a mailer, two semi-circles were die cut on the vertical sides of the piece to allow boards to be held in place, front and back, by a rubber band.

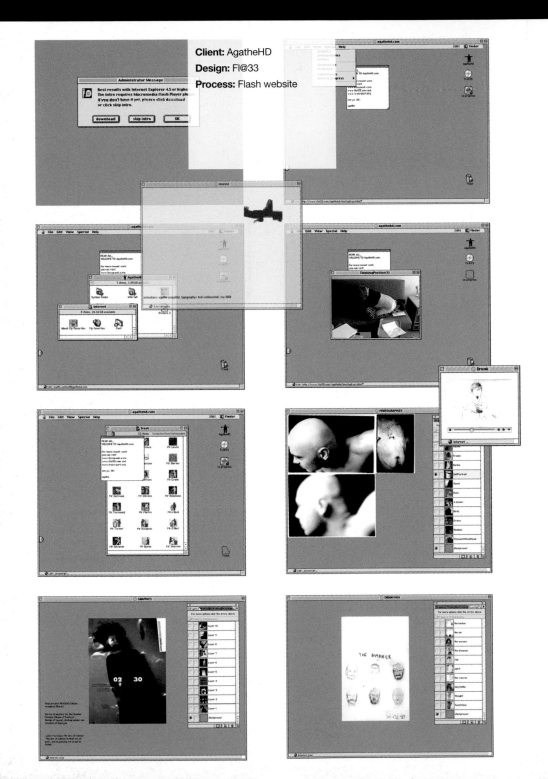

Client: AgatheHD
Design: FI@33
Process: Flash website

The Screen

Designing for the screen initially presents a number of restrictions, such as the physical area that most people will view the design at. However, the beauty of the virtual world means that there are many format aspects that can be utilised in addition to some that are unavailable to those working with physical print media.

Web page formats do not need to be restricted by screen dimensions as the designer can harness the unlimited virtual space with devices such as pop-up boxes, animations, pull-down menus, rollovers and navigation. Film formats can also mix the best of both worlds as the inherent motion of the picture means that elements can be added and taken away as necessary.

This presents the danger of creating a design overloaded with devices that could crowd and confuse, adding to the problem of communication rather than solving it, so at the root, it must be remembered that the aim is presentation of information in an effective way.

AgatheHD (left)

Appropriation and adaptation of other objects is nothing new. For her website Agathe Jacquillat took the appearance of the Macintosh operating system as her inspiration and used it as the basis of her design. When viewed on a Macintosh, this creates a 'screen' within the screen. The appropriation of the visual appearance of software is also used elsewhere in the site as the portfolio section is designed to look like the layers palette in Photoshop.
www.agatheHD.com

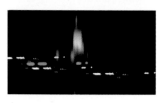

Client: Virgin
Design: Why Not Associates
Process: Post-produced
16mm film footage

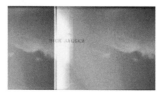

Virgin

Why Not Associates decided against industry standard film equipment to shoot an ident for Virgin Special Projects, preferring to use 16mm instead. This film format has its own unique aesthetic that imparts into the subject matter a vibrant grittiness akin to a road movie. This was enhanced with lots of post-production including overlaid type and illustration.

Format 16mm

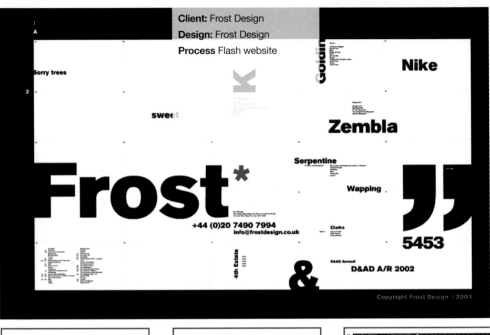

Client: Frost Design
Design: Frost Design
Process Flash website

Flash

Flash is animation software that enables web pages to be brought to life in the most remarkable ways and with a high degree of sophistication. But as with all design tools, it is possible to have too much of a good thing.

Frost Design

When using a website, a user is typically looking for a certain piece of information. Navigation is the means whereby users can be directed towards different types of information. Frost Design has chosen to mimic print media in its website design. The visual effect is more what we would expect to see on a printed page than on a website. Initially, the design looks like a poster before the Flash animation begins.

www.frostdesign.co.uk

Client: Lust
Design: Lust
Process: HTML website

Lust

The website of Lust, a typography, design and propaganda design studio based in The Hague, the Netherlands showcases Dutch graphic design. Lust has a philosophy that revolves around process-based design, coincidence, and the degradation of form and content. In one section of its website, Lust formats the screen into four windows with standard clickable links in each that change the information presented in all four windows in a manner that is definitely not standard.
www.lust.nl

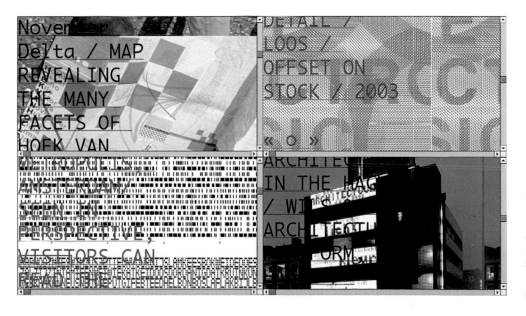

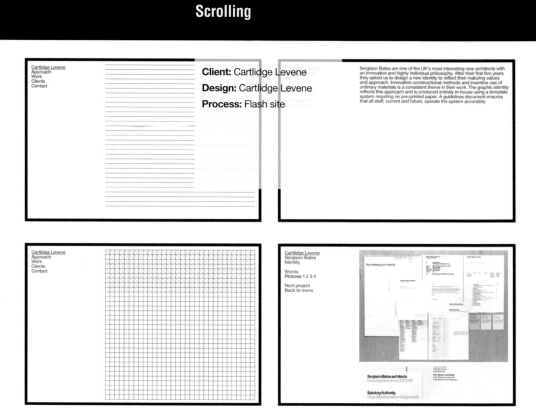

Client: Cartlidge Levene

Design: Cartlidge Levene

Process: Flash site

Sergison Bates are one of the UK's most interesting new architects with an innovative and highly individual philosophy. After their first five years they asked us to design a new identity to reflect their maturing values and approach. Innovative constructional methods and inventive use of ordinary materials is a consistent theme in their work. The graphic identity reflects this approach and is produced entirely in-house using a template system requiring no pre-printed paper. A guidelines document ensures that all staff, current and future, operate the system accurately.

Cartlidge Levene

Cartlidge Levene, a renowned modernist typographic studio, designed a Flash website for itself in which the main window displays a slither of the subsequent page as well as the current page. For example, in the portfolio section of the website, in addition to viewing an image you can see part of the next image as well. This controlled scroll effect is a means of changing and optimising the formatting constraints of the web browser.
www.cartlidgelevene.co.uk

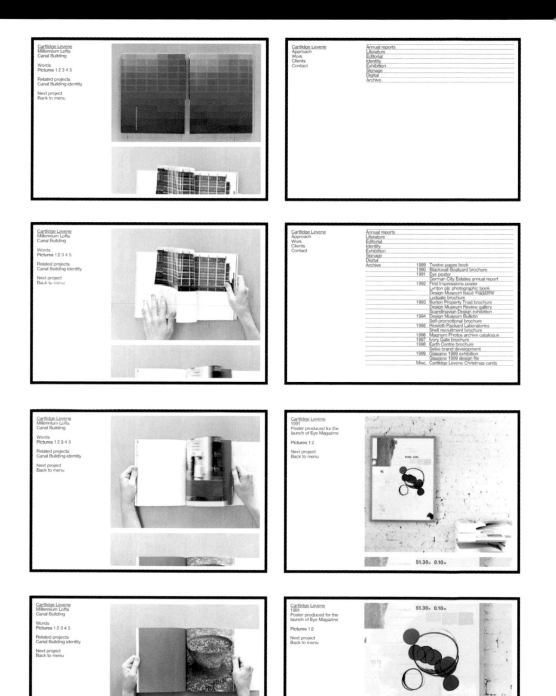

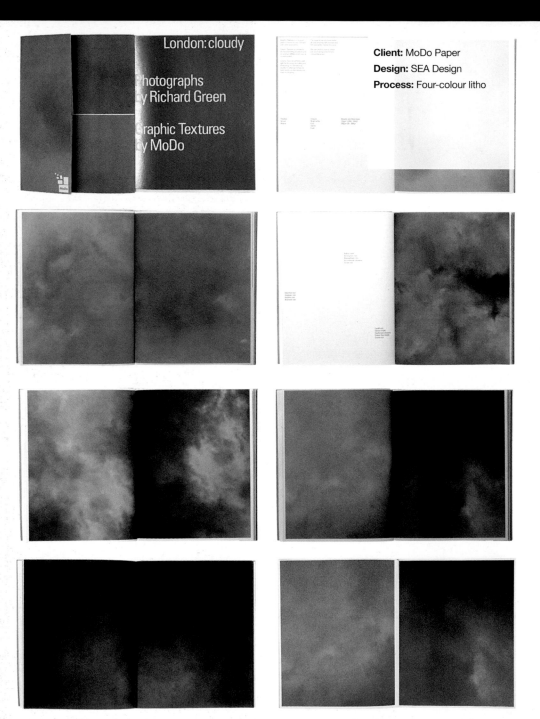

London: cloudy

Photographs by Richard Green

Graphic Textures by MoDo

Client: MoDo Paper
Design: SEA Design
Process: Four-colour litho

The Brochure

A brochure is able to combine the best elements of all the different categories. A designer can revert to the security of traditional paper sizes or embrace the full flexibility that we discussed in The Object chapter.

Although often in similar formats as books or magazines, the intention behind a brochure is quite different as their aim is to solicit positive responses to their contents. Thus it is common to see the creative use of die cuts, fold-outs, and different kinds of inserts on a variety of paper stocks.

The arrangement and separation of different types of information is frequently accomplished by the use of different formatting tools. For example, the financial pages in an annual report may be printed on a different paper stock to the chairman's discussion of the business.

As many brochures are one-off pieces designers are free to select the most appropriate format for the job, unlike book and magazine designers that may have to stick with established formats, as the examples in this section show.

MoDo Paper (left)

Designers use a wide range of substrates in brochure design to harness the diverse textures and tactile qualities available, or to benefit from the superior printability of some paper grades as this brochure called 'London: Cloudy' by SEA Design for paper manufacturer MoDo illustrates. The fine texture of the paper provides a platform that enlivens the photography of Richard Green.

Client: NESTA
Design: Hat-trick
Process: Saddle-stitched
brochure with single-colour,
self-adhesive kiss-cut cover

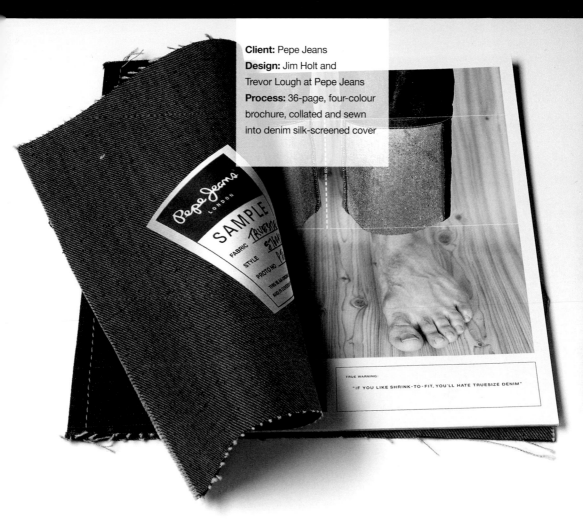

Client: Pepe Jeans
Design: Jim Holt and
Trevor Lough at Pepe Jeans
Process: 36-page, four-colour
brochure, collated and sewn
into denim silk-screened cover

TRUE WARNING:
"IF YOU LIKE SHRINK-TO-FIT, YOU'LL HATE TRUESIZE DENIM"

Pepe Jeans (above)

For this brochure for Pepe Jeans, Jim Holt and Trevor Lough stuck as close to the theme as possible by basing the design around a pair of jeans. The cover substrate is a piece of denim cloth on the inside of which is the information that is usually found on the front cover. This information is contained on a label made from the same material that the labels in the jeans are made from.

NESTA (left)

For the cover of a brochure for NESTA – the National Endowment for Science, Technology and the Arts – Hat-trick design studio used a self-adhesive substrate that was kiss cut into a number of stickers, inviting readers to distribute the 'subject to change' message each one contains.

Format Covers

Client: Bailhache Labesse
Group
Design: HGVFelton
Process: Three saddle-
stitched brochures bonded
together, high-gloss covers
with spot varnish borders

the present

Bailhache
Labesse
annual review
2002/2003

BAILHACHE

LABESSE

GROUP

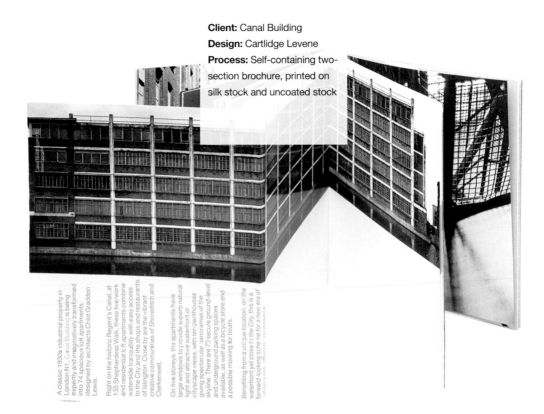

Client: Canal Building
Design: Cartlidge Levene
Process: Self-containing two-section brochure, printed on silk stock and uncoated stock

A classic 1930s industrial property in London N1, Canal Building is being expertly and imaginatively transformed into 74 spacious loft apartments designed by architects Child Graddon Lewis.

Right on the historic Regent's Canal, at 135 Shepherdess Walk, these live/work and residential loft apartments combine waterside tranquillity with easy access to the City and the shops and restaurants of Islington. Close by are the vibrant creative communities of Shoreditch and Clerkenwell.

On five storeys, the apartments have large windows to provide superb natural light and attractive waterfront or cityscape views, with ten penthouses giving spectacular panoramas of the skyline. There are 79 secure ground-level and underground parking spaces available, as well as a bicycle store and a possible mooring for boats.

Benefiting from a unique location, on the waterfront yet close to the City, this is a forward-looking scheme for a new era of

Canal Building (above)

This brochure created by Cartlidge Levene for the Canal Building in Shepherdess Walk, London is to promote the loft-style development of a formerly derelict building. It is made from two sections, one of which is 84 pages printed on a silk stock that contains commissioned imagery of the surrounding area; the other section is printed on an uncoated stock and contains building plans and other details. The last page of the first section wraps around to form a cover for the whole publication.

Bailhache Labesse Annual Review (left)

This annual review for the Bailhache Labesse Group was created by HGVFelton.'
It consists of three different-sized, saddle-stitched publications bound together that cover 'the past', 'the present' and 'the future' of the organisation and share common elements. All have high-gloss covers with a spot varnish border and use the subtle cropping of recurrent images to demonstrate the progression of time. The typography reflects the chronology of the brochures, with the past using a 'thin', the present using a 'regular' and the future using a 'bold' version of a single typeface.

Client: Focus Gallery
Design: MadeThought
Process: Wrap cover brochures with three different bellybands

Bellyband

A bellyband is a paper or plastic substrate that wraps around the 'belly' of a publication. The substrate may be a full loop or a strip. Commonly used on magazines they serve to produce an eye-catching piece of information.

Bill Brandt Exhibition Catalogue

For this catalogue for a Bill Brandt exhibition at the Focus Gallery in London, MadeThought specified that the central pages should be cut with a shorter width than the multi-panel wrap cover that encloses the work. The front cover contains information about selected works in the exhibition and folds out so that the reader can see this information as they leaf through the content pages. The exhibition brochure was produced with three different bellybands featuring key images from the exhibition.

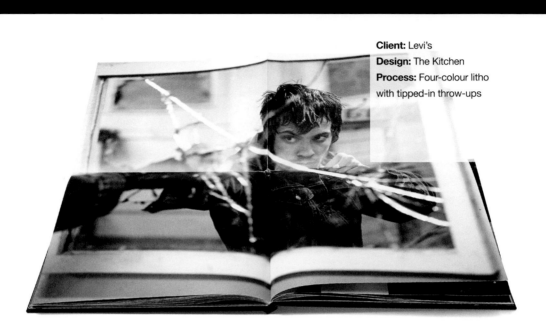

Client: Levi's
Design: The Kitchen
Process: Four-colour litho
with tipped-in throw-ups

No

Jeans manufacturer Levi's called its Denim Delinquent book *"No"* after French writer/philosopher Albert Camus who said 'a rebel is a man who says no'. To emphasise the rebellion angle The Kitchen performed a formatting rebellion of its own in the design. Spliced between the pages of the book are nine four-colour throw-ups with a French fold featuring images of rockers, tomboys and other rebellious types to add anti-authoritarian chic to the clothing line. The cover of the book is cloth bound with embossed lettering.

Throw-up
A throw-up is a substrate that is folded into a publication, typically with larger dimensions than the work that contains it, and possibly of a different stock, that is used to showcase a particular image.

Client: Plantology
Design: Iris Associates
Process: Five posters (210mm x 430mm) folded into six panels, glued together and contained between two heavy-weight foil-blocked boards

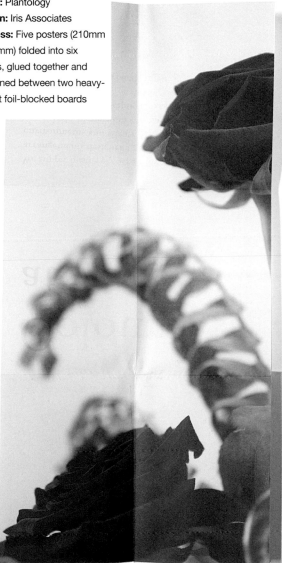

Plantology

Iris Associates designed a series of five posters, or throw-ups, that were folded into six panels for a brochure for client Plantology, a florist. The throw-ups (with one horizontal and two vertical folds) fold out to show striking flower photography. The folded posters are glued between heavyweight foil-blocked boards.

Sonneti

Using a die cut to make a series of small notches at the head and tail of the spine for this catalogue results in a distinctive bind. An elastic band stretched between the notches seals the piece, though without the degree of permanence a binding usually infers. As no folio numbers were included on the pages, the brochure can easily be taken apart and tailored to suit individual tastes.

The cover is made from a piece of board with six folds that are glued to form a spine. The size of these spine folds provides the appropriate capacity to hold the pages of the publication. Die-cut notches are found at the head and tail. The same die cut was used for the publication's pages.

Capacity

When planning a publication the designer needs to take into account the capacity of a cover to contain its pages. The dimensions of the spine will vary depending upon the number of pages in the publication. This is particularly true for perfect-bound publications and bindings like the one in the example above.

Client: Sonneti
Design: MadeThought
Process: Five-colour litho board, folded, glued with die-cut notches for elastic band binding

Spring/Summer 2002 Collections

Client: Levi's
Design: The Kitchen
Process: 16-page four-colour litho die-cut brochure with metallic cover

Levi's RED Press Brochure

The design tenet that form follows function was a challenge for The Kitchen when creating a press brochure for Levi's RED jeans given that the trend for the season in question was 'twisted'. Its solution was to individually die cut the 16 pages of the publication to create the illusion that the book is twisting as you flick through it. A metallic cover completes the piece.

Client: Corbis
Design: Segura Inc.
Process: Four-colour litho with die-cut cover

Corbis

The removal of stock via a die cut opens up a host of visual possibilities in a design. In this example for a Corbis image library catalogue, the cover is die cut with the shapes of several common objects. Laying this over the images within the catalogue shows what an image would look like as a sofa, a vase, a cup and so on, possibly opening up new avenues for image experimentation by the stock photography purchaser.

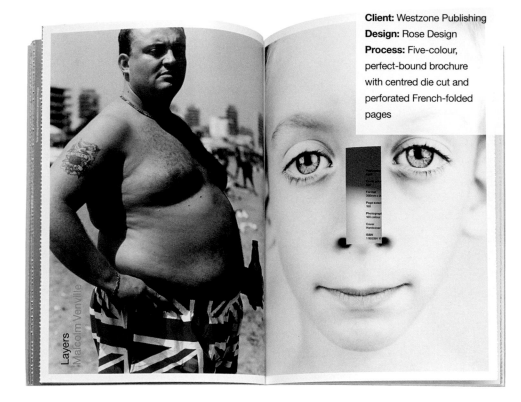

Client: Westzone Publishing
Design: Rose Design
Process: Five-colour,
perfect-bound brochure
with centred die cut and
perforated French-folded
pages

Westzone Preview Catalogue

Rose Design created this catalogue for Westzone Publishing, a company based in Venice, Italy as part of an identity to put the company firmly on the publishing map. Pictured is the preview catalogue of its titles with a die-cut aperture that gives a hint of the contents inside.

The French-folded pages are perforated on the outer edge allowing the reader to open them to discover the full 'story' the image has to tell.

French fold

A sheet of paper that is usually printed on one side and folded with two right-angle folds to form a four-page, uncut section. The section is sewn through the fold while the top edges remain folded and untrimmed.

French fold

The Image Bank

This spirit guide for
stock photography library
The Image Bank
introduces a new identity,
typographic style and
outlines for image usage.

Using French folds as a
means to organise
information, the guide
has a clear, yet engaging
narrative. The outer face
of the folded sheets
carries the main
messages of the guide,
while the inner reveals
have increasingly more
experimental
interpretations of the
typographic style.

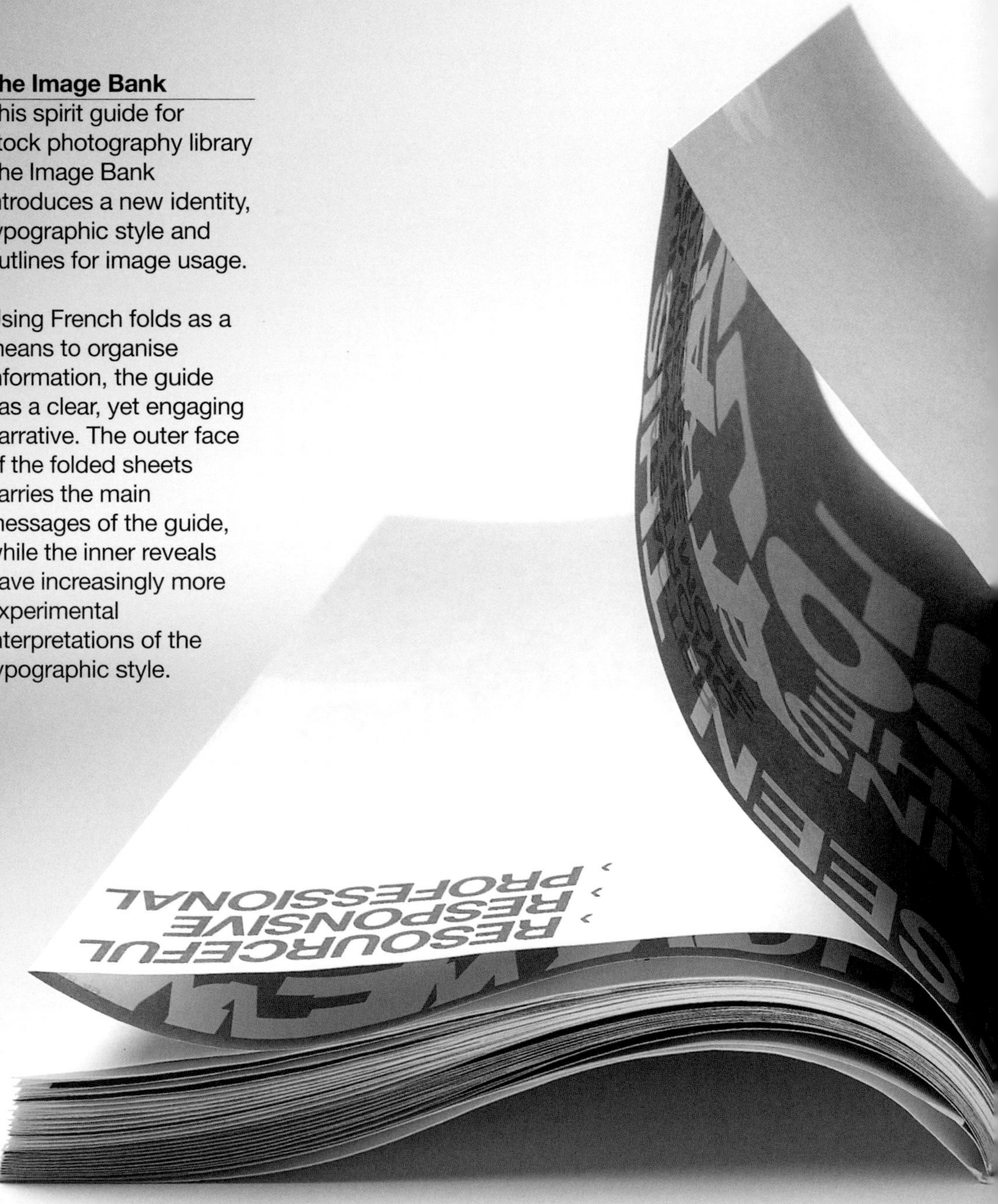

Format The Brochure

Client: The Image Bank
Design: North
Process: 74-page, French-fold
brochure, printed on thin stock
allowing showthrough

Client: Sonneti
Design: MadeThought
Process: 24-page brochure contained within four-panel wrap cover

Sonneti: Clothing Brochure

This brochure for clothing label Sonneti by MadeThought has atmospheric images of the clothing in the middle section with a four-panel wrap cover that serves as a contents page containing images of all the collection, product codes and related information.

Wrap cover
A wrap cover is a cover with more than the standard two panels. The extra panels fold back and wrap around the principal two cover panels.

Client: Arts 2000
Design: Eg.G
Process: Four-colour
litho fold-out brochure
with three-panel throw-out

Year of the Artist

For this A4 'Year of the Artist' brochure for Arts 2000 featuring photography
by Mark Harvey, design studio Eg.G included a three-panel throw-out at the
back that included perforated reply cards on the back panel flap.

'Year of the Artist' seeks to connect with the artist in everyone. This brochure
depicts a typical street scene on the reverse of which is a cut-out-and-build
interpretation of the scene allowing the reader to become an artist themselves.

Client: Gagosian Gallery
Design: Bruce Mau Design
Process: Four-colour folded brochure/poster that measures over 1.5m x 1m when opened, with perforated guides

Richard Hamilton: Products™

Richard Hamilton: Products™

Bruce Mau Design created this poster for an exhibition by pop artist Richard Hamilton at the Gagosian Gallery in London. It is a 32-panel fold-down poster that has perforated edges to help it fold. The large-format poster opens to reveal a near life-size image by Rita Donagh of the artist carrying one of his works, 'Epiphany', produced in 1964.

Client: Delta Airlines
Design: Turnbull Ripley
Process: Four-colour litho
with polypropylene case

Delta Airlines (above and below)

Rather than producing a single publication covering all elements of the sales kit for Delta airlines, Turnbull Ripley chose to break down the various components of the kit into separate publications. The resulting series comprises single publications for product offerings, bonuses and the different travel classes. This method divides (sometimes complex) information into easily managed blocks.

Paul Smith Catalogue (right)

This catalogue for fashion designer Paul Smith is based on a children's card game of matching objects with their names. A series of cards featuring products and accompanying name plaques offers a playful randomness to the order.

tie s...

tea pot

Client: Paul Smith
Design: Aboud Sodano
Process: Four-colour cards
cut into two different sizes

hat

umbre...

painting

braces

Client: Crafts Council
Design: NB: Studio
Process: Heavy laminated board cover that is creased, folded and glued. Contains a 28-page saddle-stitched booklet

Jerwood Applied Arts Prize 2003

This brochure for the Crafts Council has a heavy laminated board for the cover that is folded back on itself and glued. Two vertical parallel creases form a spine.

Laminate

A laminate is a stock made by bonding two or more layers of stock together. Typically used to provide a thick cover stock comprising a cheaper inner with a printable outer.

Client: McNaughton Paper
Design: Radley Yeldar
Process: 17-page loose-leaf sheet brochure with tracing paper dust-jacket

Zanders T2000

To demonstrate the ability to print on a new high quality transparent paper, Radley Yeldar created this brochure for paper company McNaughton.

The design uses the transparency of the stock to juxtapose an image printed in orange on to photographs by John Edwards that appear on facing pages: by turning the trace link page a jelly mould becomes a swimmer's hat, a tightrope becomes a washing line and a candle's flame becomes a water droplet.

Format Stocks

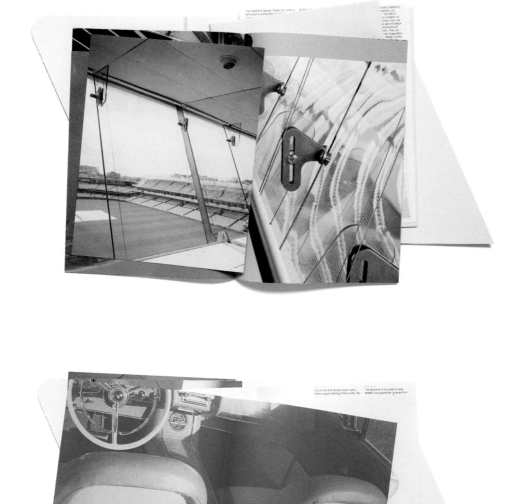

Client: Lord's cricket ground
Design: Cartlidge Levene
Process: Four-colour,
cut board cover containing
four-colour inserts

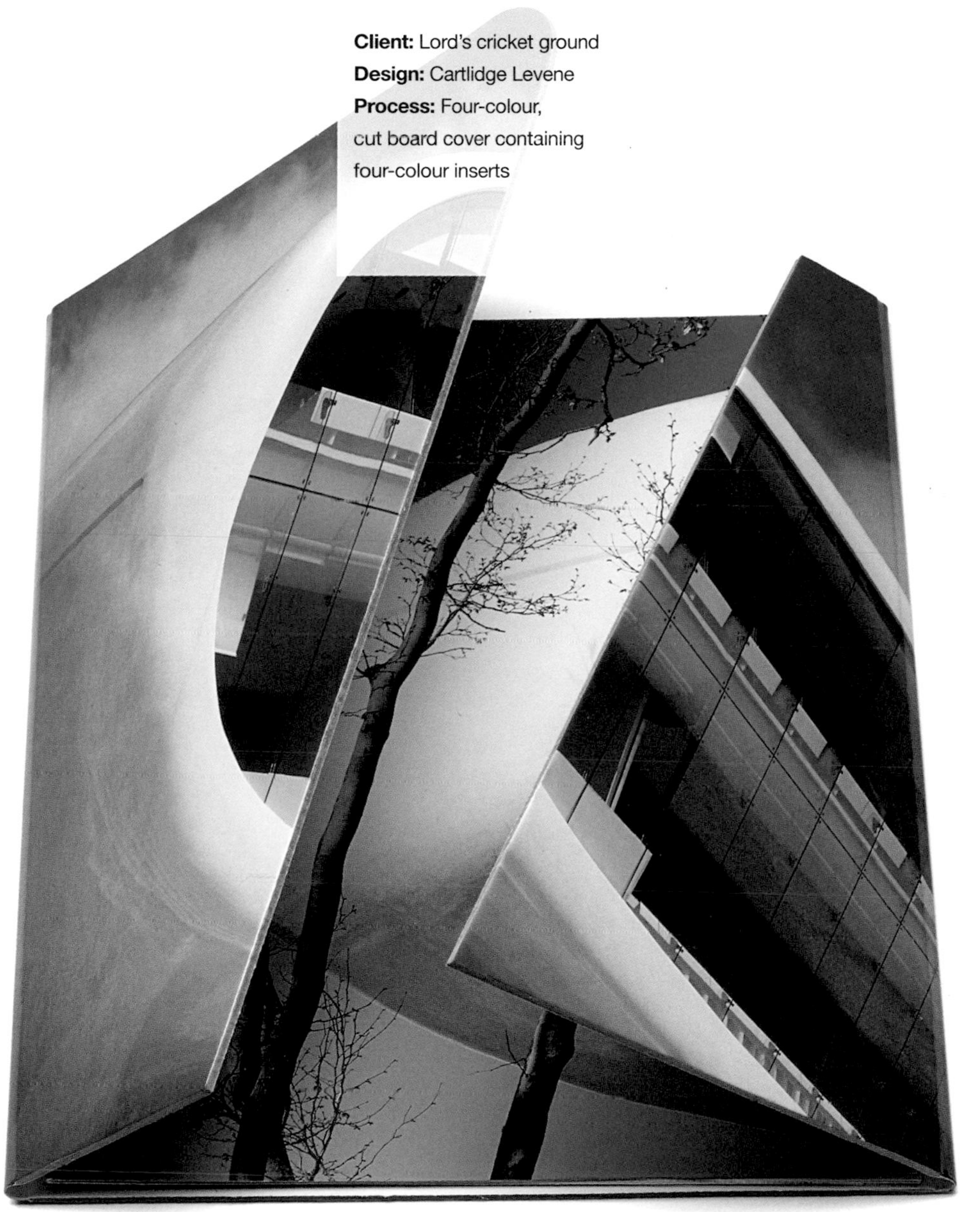

NatWest Media Centre Brochure

This is a brochure for a building at the Lord's cricket ground in London by Future Systems. Cartlidge Levene designed a thick covered board that forms a folder with a diagonal cut for an opening that wraps around the two sections that comprise the main body. Inside are two loose-leaf sections; one provides a photographic record of the construction project, while the other provides background information about it.

Format Stocks

Tip-ins

A tip-in is a means to attach an insert into a book or magazine by gluing along the binding edge. It is a method for attaching individual elements into the publication such as colour plates, that are typically produced on a different stock, where insufficient pages will be produced to warrant the printing of a separate section.

Client: Manhattan
Loft Corporation
Design: North
Process: Six-colour
brochure using various
stocks tipped-in to
main body

View

North used seven stocks to produce a *mélange* of textures for this brochure
celebrating ten years of property developer Manhattan Loft Corporation. The
publication is based around the colour plates set in white frames that contain
commissioned photography of the area. The frames are separated by translucent
tip-ins. Undersized tip-ins of a heavier stock are used to provide additional
reference information and atmospheric imagery.

All the tip-ins bind from the same edge (the bottom in this case) of the book,
which is a usual requirement when collating and binding.

Client: Paul Smith
Design: Aboud Sodano
Process: Four-colour cards
in die-cut presentation box

Paul Smith Brochure (above)

This brochure/point-of-sale piece for Paul Smith's children's collection is a box that has a die-cut semicircle in the front. The box contains loose-leaf cards of children wearing items from the clothing range that can be slotted into the aperture and thus displayed.

4th Estate (right)

Frost Design created a brochure without binding and without a cover for this catalogue for book publisher 4th Estate. The heavyweight, loose-leaf cards have been letterpressed and are presented in a storage box. The stock choice provides greater durability, an important consideration given that the pages are loose-leaf.

Client: 4th Estate Books
Design: Frost Design
Process: 42 loose-leaf boards, letterpressed both sides and sealed in a card box

HELP LINE
Faye Sultan

THE SHELL
Jane Thy

THE S
Ross

MY TINY LIFE
Julian

BARRA
Eileer

THE GUARDIAN CAREERS GUIDES

An essential series of modern guides for today's job market, backed and prompted by the No. 1 brand in recruitment. Lively and up-to-date, the series is driven by the recognition that career planning is more flexible, less certain and more in the hands of the individual than ever before.

SECONDARY EDUCATION
Kathy Vandyck

The government's pledge to reduce class sizes means that recruitment in secondary education will be intensive over the next couple of years. This guide examines likely openings in every subject area, while highlighting the growing need for management and analytical abilities among teachers faced by the financial pressures and competition of league tables.

£8.99 August
Paperback Original
216 x 135mm 160pp
1 85702 750 7
World
US, translation, serial, film/TV, radio reading: Fourth Estate

ACCOUNTANCY
Sarah Perrin

Traditionally seen as one of the least exciting but safest career areas, accountancy skills are now required in all manner of businesses from the city to charities, schools and hospitals. This book explains the enviable range of options from working for a professional partnership to climb the corporate ladder; from working in the public sector to self-empl

£8.99 August
Paperback Original
216 x 135mm 160pp
1 85702 751 5
World
US, translation, serial, film/TV, radio reading: Fourth Estate

Format Loose-leaf

Client: Capital Commitment
Design: Hat-trick
Process: Four-colour litho, foil-blocked covers; embossed box with spot varnish

30 Gresham Street Sales Brochure

This sales brochure for a new building at 30 Gresham Street, London was designed by Hat-trick. The work uses the number 30 throughout: the lid has 30 words that are integral to the values of the development embossed on it, with the first line also having a spot varnish. The box contains the building plans with 30 embossed on the cover. It also contains two half-sized brochures with 30 foil-blocked on the covers. One brochure contains 30 words and the other contains 30 accompanying images. There is also a series of guides covering '30 points of view', '30 minutes around Gresham Street', '30 illustrious neighbours' and a map with '30 ways to Gresham Street'. With the marketing of real-estate, taking ownership of an address has distinct advantages. Potential buyers/leasers begin to see the building as an important part of an already important street.

Client: Doric
Design: Roundel
Process: Product brochure
with throw-ups, gatefolds
and inserted letterhead

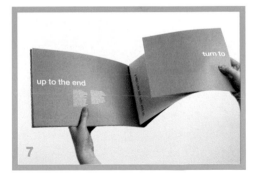

Doric

This poster/brochure, entitled 'turn to',
uses written instructions that tell the
reader how to unfold the product.
Completion of each instruction reveals
another page, gatefold or throw-up.
The final instruction, 'turn to', reveals
a letterheaded note that uses the
same visual language-'On your right
you can't miss it'- pointing to the
addressee of the letter.

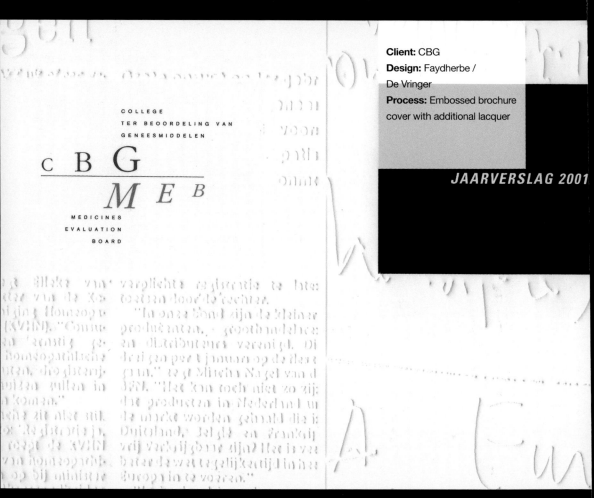

Client: CBG
Design: Faydherbe / De Vringer
Process: Embossed brochure cover with additional lacquer

CBG

The subtle tone-on-tone effect that can be produced by embossing is a key part of this design by Faydherbe / De Vringer for the Netherlands' CBG Medicines Evaluation Board annual report.

The embossing technique is used in a very different way to its normal role of simply providing a tactile dimension to emphasise an aspect of a design.

Faydherbe / De Vringer wanted a pure and plain design in terms of colour, but without the lack of colour preventing complexity. The use of embossing meant that they could create a detailed, textured design with minimal use of colour. So that the colour areas of the cover could be easily distinguished and read, they were given an extra layer of lacquer to provide extra definition.

A contrasting effect was used for the body of the report with a switch to black pages with silver text.

Embossing and debossing

An emboss is a design stamped into a substrate without ink or foil resulting in a raised surface. When a stamp is used to give a recessed surface, the process is called debossing. The two processes are used to give decorative, textured effects to a publication and are typically used to provide emphasis to certain elements of the design. An emboss used on an uninked area is sometimes called blind embossing, an example of which can be seen opposite for the CBG publication.

Client: Issey Miyake
Design: Research Studios
Process: Four-colour, die-cut brochure with loose-leaf insert

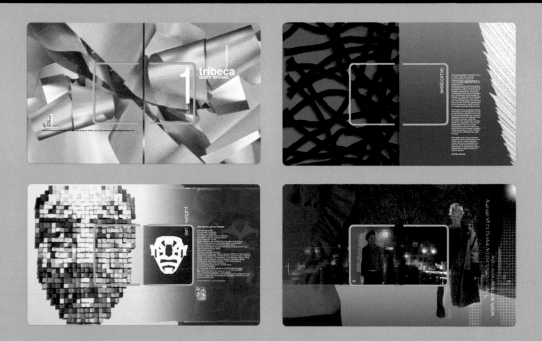

Issey Miyake

Research Studios used a subtle but effective die cut for this brochure for the tribeca Issey Miyake store in New York. The brochure has a central die cut that gives two 'U' shapes either side of the spine (the silver brackets that can be seen in the images). These provide a physical separation by creating a small book within the pages of the larger piece so that a reader can flip through either section independently. The work included a loose-leaf contents page, shown below right, and was protected by an embossed outer sleeve, below left.

Artists, musicians and designers were commissioned to show pieces alongside the brands within the store and this juxtaposition is maintained in the brochure.

Format Dual narrative

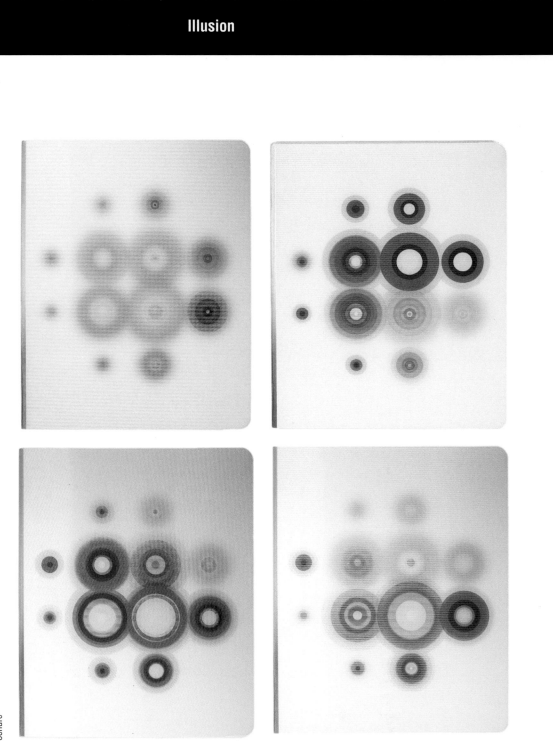

Client: Telewest
Design: North
Process: 124-page book,
die-cut corners, lenticular
cover front and back

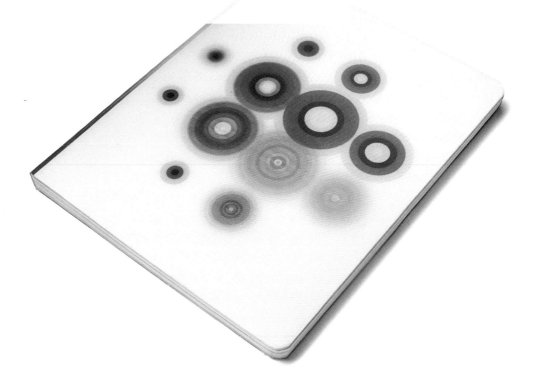

Telewest Identity Programme

Design studio North put a lenticular image on the front and rear covers of the
Design Guidelines Brand Manual for Telewest. The cover image is the organisation's
logo that moves and changes as the reader changes his or her viewing angle. This
ties in with an animated version of the logo that appears in television commercials
for the organisation. The idea is very simple but well executed.

Lenticular
A lenticular is a printed image that shows depth or motion as the viewing angle changes.

Format Illusion

Client: Esther Franklin
Design: MadeThought
Process: Four four-colour
sections, four spot varnish
black page inserts, saddle-
stitched cover, also spot
varnished and cut short

Esther Franklin

Format is frequently used as a device or keystone for other design elements such as layout, as this example by MadeThought for client Esther Franklin illustrates. The cover of the brochure is cut short both horizontally and vertically and this is used as a template for the grid into which photographs by Nino Munoz are laid out. The photographs are printed to the dimensions of the cover so that the border of the page, the missing space of the cover, shows another image surrounding the main image. This results in the illusion that there is another page underneath. In fact, all this is printed on one page. The cover and intermediate pages are printed with a varnish to give a shiny black on matt black effect.

Client: Bristol Regeneration Partnership
Design: Thirteen
Process: Silk-screened greyboard outer cover that doubles as envelope

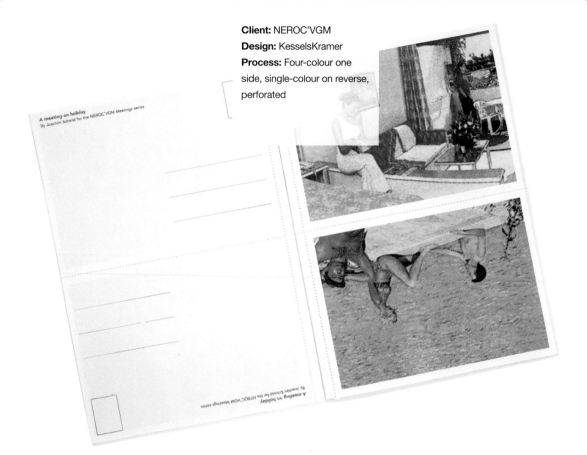

Client: NEROC'VGM
Design: KesselsKramer
Process: Four-colour one side, single-colour on reverse, perforated

A Meeting on Holiday, Postcardland (above)

This is a book designed by KesselsKramer for the NEROC'VGM series of books by artists exploring the theme of meeting featuring 'A Meeting on Holiday, Postcardland', by Joachim Schmid. Schmid sifted through thousands of images and arranged the ones in this book into a kind of visual poetry. Each page has a series of circular perforations through the middle and up the spine edge so the images become tear-out postcards.

Bristol Regeneration Partnership (left)

This 2001/2 annual report for the Bristol Regeneration Partnership designed by Thirteen is an A5-format book stitched into its own mailable self-sealing greyboard envelope to reduce postage costs. Upon receipt, the top and bottom flaps can be removed as they are perforated, so the object sheds its postal skin and functions as a book.

Format Perforation

Client: CTD Capita Digital
Design: Hat-trick
Process: Printed one side only, bound by a bolt, with a laminated cover

Indichrome System Introduction Guide

This design for a guide to the new Indichrome printing system is based on the Pantone colour swatch book. The printing system produces colours that are more accurate than previous digital printing services. This accuracy is highlighted in the design by printing the 'names' of various colour hues and intensities in their respective colours. Rather than being able to simply print a 'purple' you can print various purple variants such as HAZE, RAIN, PATCH, DEEP, HEART and so on.

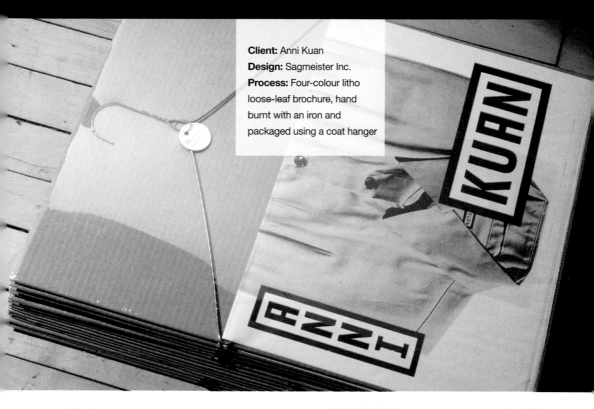

Client: Anni Kuan
Design: Sagmeister Inc.
Process: Four-colour litho loose-leaf brochure, hand burnt with an iron and packaged using a coat hanger

Anni Kuan Brochure

The fashion world pursues the unique to catch the eye and differentiate, and that is exactly what Anni Kuan, a New York fashion designer, got from Sagmeister Inc. – a loose broadsheet brochure that hangs on a wire coat hanger. Each page has been subjected to some unique print finishing – by being burnt with an iron! Apparently it took five minutes to burn each of the brochure's 16 pages.

Format Print finishing

Client: Underware
Design: Faydherbe /
De Vringer
Process: Flock cover with
foil-blocked type and image

dolly

Dolly Typeface Catalogue

'Dolly' is an alternative typeface catalogue for a new typeface called 'Dolly' designed by Underware. Dolly is also the name of the dog character that is the product's logo foil-blocked on to the cover of this catalogue designed by Faydherbe / De Vringer and the protagonist of the catalogue's storyline.

Flock was chosen for the cover, a substrate that can take a foil-blocked logo and that is sufficiently robust to be die cut to house the CD holder. The effect of the textless, foil-stamped front cover is dramatic and intriguing.

Flock

This is paper coated with flock – very fine woollen refuse or vegetable fibre dust – that is fixed with glue or size to give the substrate a velvety or cloth-like appearance.

Foil stamp

A foil stamp is a foil or coloured tape that is pressed on to a substrate using heat and pressure.

ABCDEFGHIJKLMNOP
QRSTUVWXYZŒÆÇ &
abcdefghijklmnopq
rstuvwxyzœæç
{0123456789}
(fiflß);:[¶]?!*
àáäâãàèéëêùúüû
òóöôøõñ
"$£€ƒ¢" «©†@»

Dolly Roman

ABCDEFGHIJKLMNOP
QRSTUVWXYZŒÆÇ &
abcdefghijklmnopq
rstuvwxyzœæç
{0123456789}
*(fiflß);:[¶]?!**
àáäâãàèéëêùúüû
òóöôøõñ
"$£€ƒ¢" «©†@»

Dolly Italic

Client: Hans Brinker
Budget Hotel
Design: KesselsKramer
Process: Perfect-bound four-
colour brochure with centred
cross-cut pages

Check In / Check Out Book

This brochure for the Hans Brinker Budget Hotel in Amsterdam, the Netherlands by KesselsKramer has pages cut through the middle to create separate components that can be independently flipped, under a flock cover. The theme of the imagery is that the guests are fine when they arrive but look the worse for wear when they leave having had such a good time in Amsterdam. The separation allows an interactive juxtaposition of before-and-after images.

Format Flock

Client: Onitsuka

Design: Eg.G

Process: Japanese-bound, loose-leaf French-fold booklet with flock cover

Japanese binding

Japanese or stab binding is a binding method whereby the pages are sewn together with one continual thread.

Onitsuka

This brochure for Onitsuka clothing company by Eg.G uses a Japanese binding to provide a decorative element to the flock cover, both elements reflect the cloth trade the client is involved in.

Client: Hub
Design: NB: Studio
Process: 148-page catalogue printed on to a stock coated one side and uncoated on the reverse. Left with an open bind

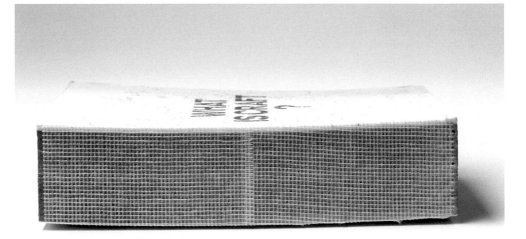

Hub

This catalogue by NB: Studio for Hub, the centre for craft design and making is essentially a series of heavyweight postcards bound into a book format. In addition, no cover is applied to the spine, creating a sculptural appearance and feel to the publication.

Flexible Furniture

To illustrate how an innovative piece of flexible furniture works designer John Rushworth did not stop at a brochure showing photos of the piece of furniture in its various positions. Instead, in this piece for the Crafts Council, he perforated the back page containing the photos so readers could separate and arrange them in the correct order and bind them with an elastic band to create a flip book that animates the furniture. The colour scheme for the exhibition catalogue was inspired by some of the key pieces in it.

Animation

Whether on computer, in film or cartoons, animation is typically produced from a series of still images each subtly different from the previous that when viewed at speed create the effect of movement.

Client: Crafts Council
Design: Pentagram
(John Rushworth)
Process: Perforated brochure
that can be reconstructed into
a flip book

13a

Glossary

As we have explained some of the physical techniques that can be manipulated in design, we have introduced many specialist terms. These are collected together in the following glossary to provide an easy reference section. While it is impossible to be exhaustive, we have provided the most common terms used by the printing and publishing industry in relation to format.

As you will notice, these pages are printed as a separate section on an uncoated, coloured stock called Kraft, which provides a further example of how the use of different stocks can provide a physical separation for different parts of a publication.

Client: Katy Ingram
Design: Turnbull Ripley
Process: 12-panel accordion-
fold brochure with self-cover

Katy Ingram

In this example of a concertina fold, Turnbull Ripley provide a physical separation for two distinct but related ideas for a promotional piece called 'Can You See It?' On one side the artist's thoughts, ideas and influences are printed, with the finished works appearing on the other. In this instance the fold allows the side-by-side positioning of information on each side yet keeps them separated in a manner that cannot be so effectively achieved with a booklet.

Accordion or concertina fold
Two or more parallel folds that go in opposite directions and open out like an accordion.

A series paper sizes
ISO metric standard paper size based on the square root of two ratio. The A0 sheet (841mm x 1189mm) is one square metre and each size (A1, A2, A3, A4 etc.) thereafter differs from the next by a factor of either 2 or ½.

Basis weight
The weight, measured in pounds, of 500 sheets (a ream) of paper cut to a standard size.

Bellyband
A printed band that wraps around a publication; typically used with magazines.

Bible paper or India paper
A thin, lightweight, long-life, opaque paper grade typically made from 25% cotton and linen rags or flax with chemical wood pulp, named after its most common usage.

Binding
Any of several processes for holding together the pages or sections of a publication to form a book, magazine, brochure or some other format using stitches, wire, glue or other media.

Binding screws
Used with the Purdue hard cover binding method to secure a front and back cover to the pages.

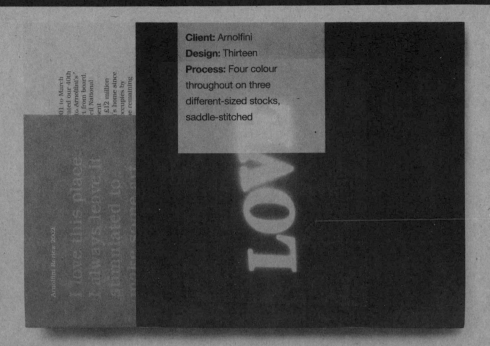

Client: Arnolfini
Design: Thirteen
Process: Four colour throughout on three different-sized stocks, saddle-stitched

Arnolfini

For the annual review for Bristol art organisation Arnolfini, Thirteen created a saddle-stitched brochure using stocks of different sizes in both height and width dimensions. The standard sized pages were used for the body of the report and the odd-sized pages were used for displaying images and quotations.

Bleed printing

When the printed information extends past where the page will be trimmed so that the colours or images continue to the edge of the cut page.

Bolt

An item that holds a series of loose pages together in the corner. For example, a Pantone swatch is held with a bolt.

Brittleness

Meaning easily broken, an important paper attribute to be aware of when considering folding as you do not want it to crack.

B series paper sizes

ISO metric standard paper size based on the square root of two ratio. B sizes are intermediate sizes to the A series sizes.

Buckram

A coarse linen or cotton fabric sized with glue or gum, used for covering a hard-cover binding.

Burst binding

At the folding stage the sections are perforated on the binding side to allow glue to penetrate into each fold of paper. The glued spine then has a cover applied and wrapped around the book block.

Canadian binding

Essentially a spiral-bound volume with a wraparound cover that can stand up better on a shelf, with a spine for the title. A half-Canadian has an exposed spiral, a full Canadian does not.

Case or edition binding

A common hard-cover book-binding method that sews signatures together, flattens the spine, applies endsheets and

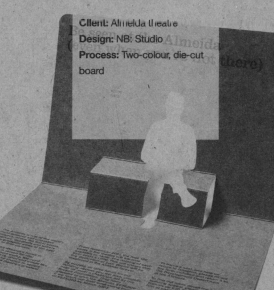

Client: Almeida theatre
Design: NB: Studio
Process: Two-colour, die-cut board

Almeida Theatre

This is a fundraising invite for the Almeida Theatre in Islington, London asking people for a donation in return for the donor's name being placed on a theatre seat. Two die cuts at a right angle to the central creased fold turn an empty space into a seat creating the silhouette of a man.

head and tail bands to the spine. Hard covers are attached, the spine is usually rounded and grooves along the cover edge act as hinges.

C-fold
Six panels are formed with two parallel folds in a spiral fold configuration. The final page nests inside the pocket created by the other fold and is usually slightly narrower than the other panels.

Concertina fold
See Accordion fold.

Crack-back
A backing stock with a self-adhesive coating that may have a die cut to make it easier to peel away from the stock it backs.

Creasing
A process using a blade and pressure to impart a crease into a substrate so that it can subsequently be folded. Similar to a die cut except the blade does not penetrate the substrate.

Creep
Creep occurs in a saddle-stitched publication when the bulk of the paper causes the inner pages to extend (creep) further than the outer pages when folded.

Cross fold
Two or more folds going in different directions, typically at right angles. Mainly used in book work where paper is cross folded and cut to form a signature.

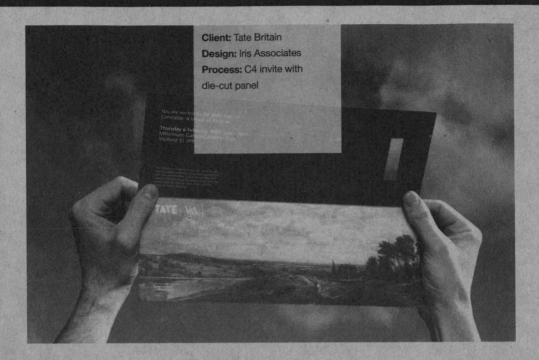

Client: Tate Britain
Design: Iris Associates
Process: C4 invite with die-cut panel

You are invited to the press view of
Constable: A breath of fresh air

Thursday 6 February 2003 10am–3pm
Millennium Galleries, Arundel Gate
Sheffield S1 2PP

Constable: A Breath of Fresh Air

The invite for an exhibition entitled 'Constable: A Breath of Fresh Air' at Tate Britain in Liverpool included a die cut to create an aperture. When the invite is folded this aperture reveals part of a landscape by English painter John Constable.

Deboss
As emboss but recessed into the substrate.

Deckle or feather edge
This is the ragged edge of the paper as it comes from the papermaking machine. Machine-made paper has two deckle edges, handmade has four. When not cut off it can serve a decorative purpose. An imitation deckle edge can be created by tearing the edge of the paper.

Die cut
Special shapes cut in a substrate by a steel die.

Double gatefold
Three panels that fold into the middle of a publication. These are slightly smaller in width to the inner panels so that when folded they can nest properly inside the publication.

Duotone
A duotone is a two-colour reproduction from a monochrome original.

Dust-jacket
A jacket around a hardback publication that originally offered protection against dirt and dust, as the name suggests, but more recently has become an integral graphic extension of the book and a key device for promotion.

Emboss
A design stamped without ink or foil giving a raised surface.

Endpaper or endsheets
The heavy cartridge paper pages at the front and back of a hardback book that join the book

Client: Luke Morgan
Design: Studio Myerscough
Process: Four-colour litho on
to DL envelope

Luke Morgan
This invitation for a Luke Morgan event features a print of the back of a car, making a rather dramatic statement on an unusual substrate.

block to the hardback binding. Sometimes feature maps, a decorative colour or design.
Envelope
An object that can be made from a variety of different stocks that is used to contain and post letters, brochures and other printed matter.
Extent
The number of pages in a book.
Fan fold
A fan fold or accordion fold is a series of parallel folds made in the opposite direction to the previous

fold along its length and then one right-angle fold to create a fan.
Flash
Animation software that enables web pages to be brought to life in the most remarkable ways and with a high degree of sophistication.
Flock
A speciality cover paper produced by coating the sheet with size in patterns or all over, after which a dyed flock powder (very fine woollen refuse or vegetable fibre dust) is applied. Originally

intended to simulate tapestry and Italian velvet brocade.
Flood colour
A term referring to the colour fill of an item.
Foil, heat or hot stamp
Foil pressed on to a substrate using heat and pressure. Also known as block print or foil emboss.
Folio or page
A sheet of paper folded in half is a folio and each half of the folio is one page. A single folio has four pages.

Format Glossary

Client: Ivory Gate Ltd.
Design: Studio Myerscough
Process: Die-cut bookmark in
four-colour brochure

66 St John Street

This book for refurbished apartments at 66 St John Street in London was designed by Studio Myerscough. Surreal images such as sunflowers and penguins are used on a bookmark that has been die cut to the outline of the building's shape. It provides a contrast with the more traditionally informative elements, building plans and alike, that are contained under a series of gatefolds.

French fold
A sheet of paper that is only printed on one side and folded with two right-angle folds to form a four-page, uncut section. The section is sewn through the fold while the top edges remain folded and untrimmed.

Frontispiece
An illustration inserted to face the title page.

Gatefold
The left and right edges fold inward with parallel folds and meet in the middle of the page

without overlapping.

Grain
Paper grain is the direction in which most of its fibres lay and is determined during the papermaking process. The grain flows in the direction that the paper passes through the papermaking machine.

Headband
A headband is a piece of cloth tape that covers the top or bottom of the spine. It is both decorative and provides protection to the spine.

Imposition
The arrangement of pages in the sequence and position they will appear when printed before being cut, folded and trimmed.

International Paper Sizes (ISO)
A range of standard metric paper sizes.

Japanese or stab binding
A binding method whereby the pages are sewn together with one continual thread.

Client: Levi's
Design: KesselsKramer
Process: Single-colour booklet
containing folded and saddle-
stitched single-colour poster

Levi's Music Job Club

This small booklet for clothing label Levi's contains a folded poster that has been saddle-stitched inside, but can be removed. The poster and booklet are lacquered giving a high-gloss sheen.

Kiss cut
A method of die cutting whereby the face material of a self-adhesive substrate is die cut but not completely through to the backing sheet. This enables the face material to be easily removed from the backing sheet.

Lacquer
A coating applied to a printed work to provide a high-gloss finish.

Laminate
A laminate is a stock made by bonding two or more layers of stock together. Typically used to provide a thick cover stock comprising a cheap inner with a printable outer.

Lenticular
A printed image that shows depth or motion as the viewing angle changes.

Loose-leaf binding
A binding method in which individual, punched sheets are loosely held by a binder.

Litho
A printing technique in which the ink is transferred from a printing plate to a 'blanket' cylinder and then to the paper or material on which it is to be printed.

Micro-printing
A specialist printing technique for reproducing exceptionally fine levels of detail.

Modernism
An artistic style emphasising functionality and progress to move beyond the external physical representation of reality.

Format Glossary

Client: Black Dog Publishing
Design: Gavin Ambrose
Process: Tessellating
book jacket

Metis – Urban Cartographies

In this design for Black Dog Publishing the cover tessellates and can only be seen in full when four copies of the book are placed together. The image is intentionally far too big for the format of an individual book but, thus displayed, would attract more attention at the point of sale.

Perfect binding
A binding method commonly used for paperback books where the signatures are held together with a flexible adhesive that also attaches a paper cover to the spine. The fore edge is trimmed flat.

Perforation
A series of cuts or holes manufactured on a form to weaken it for tearing.

Post-modernism
A philosophy that questions the notion that there is a reliable reality by deconstructing the established order of things.

Purdue binding
A hard cover is placed on the top and bottom of the folios and three holes are drilled along the binding edge into which binding screws are placed. A cloth is then wrapped around the spine.

Ream
500 sheets of paper.

Recto/Verso
The pages of an open book with recto being the right-hand page and verso the left-hand.

Saddle-stitching
A binding method used for booklets, programmes and small catalogues. Signatures are nested and wire stitches are applied through the spine along the centrefold. When opened, saddle-stitched books lay flat.

Client: Kaap Helder

Design: KesselsKramer

Process: Open binding with half-size greyboard cover glued to the outer of the text block

Kaap Helder

For the Kaap Helder art exhibition held at the former naval dockyard Oude Rijkserf Willemsoord in the Netherlands, KesselsKramer used an open binding with a half-size greyboard cover glued to the outer that produces an interesting, half-finished effect.

Sewn section

Unbound book block that has had its binding edge sewn. The blocks are then sewn together.

Showthrough or strikethrough

Where printing inks can be seen through the substrate on the reverse of the page. Particularly common with thin paper stocks and/or those with low loadings of fillers and coating; it is generally undesirable.

Side-stitching

A binding method for publications that are too bulky for saddle-stitching. Signatures are collated, placed flat under the stitching head and stapled. Side-stitched items do not lay flat when open.

Signature or section

A signature or section is a sheet of paper folded to form several pages which are collected together for binding.

Slipcase

A protective case for a book or set of books open at one end so that only the book spines are visible.

Spiral fold

A substrate has two or more parallel folds that fold in on each other from the left or right. The final page is usually slightly narrower than the others to allow it to nest properly inside the pocket created by the other fold.

Client: Natalie Imbruglia
Design: Form Design
Process: CD packaging
with deckle edge

Torn

This CD cover format by Form Design for Natalie Imbruglia's single 'Torn' visually represents the song's title with the top of the picture having a deckle edge to appear as though it has been torn off. This may be achieved naturally during the papermaking process or artificially by tearing the paper edge.

Spot varnish
The application of varnish to a specific area of a printed piece.

Stock
The paper to be printed upon.

Substrate
The material or surface to be printed upon.

Surrealism
A style of art and literature developed in the 20th century that stressed the subconscious or non-rational significance of imagery arrived at by automatism or the exploitation of chance

effects and incongruous juxtapositions.

Tailband
A decorative strip of coloured material glued to the bottom of a book block spine of a hardback book. Always used with a headband.

Throw-up
A sheet of paper that is folded and bound into a publication such that it can be opened out to a much larger dimension than the publication that contains it.

Tip-in
To attach an insert in a book or magazine by gluing along the binding edge such as to tip-in a colour plate.

Transfer or decal
A design on a substrate that is intended to be transferred to the surface of another substrate, usually glass, wood, metal or ceramic.

Client: Esprit Europe
Design: HGVFelton
Process: Five single A4 leaves wiro bound with 12 short varnished tip-ins in between heavy uncoated cover stock

Esprit Europe

This wiro-bound brochure has five A4 leaves with 12 short varnished tip-ins between heavy uncoated cover stock. The imagery of the tipped-in elements is based on the Solari analogue information display system common in airports and train stations to convey messages. The rich, atmospheric black-and-white imagery draws attention to the spine of the publication where the wiro binding is used as the hinge in the message system that readers are invited to interact with.

Unsewn binding
See Perfect binding.

UV coating
Coating applied to a printed substrate that is bonded and cured with ultraviolet light.

Varnish
A clear or tinted liquid shellac or plastic coating put on a printed piece to add a glossy, satin or dull finish applied like a final ink layer after a piece is printed (see front cover).

Vellum
Vellum is commonly used to mean a translucent paper although it can also mean a slightly rough paper finish.

Wiro/comb binding
A spine of plastic or wire rings that binds a document and allows it to open flat.

Z-bind
A 'z' shaped cover that is used to join two separate publications.

Z-fold
See Accordion fold.

Conclusion

In this volume we have attempted to show how leading contemporary designers use format to enhance and augment their designs. Being innovative with the physical properties of a piece can result in something as eye-catching as can be produced through the use of colour, images, typography, and layout.

Tweaking the physical aspects can provide a much larger surface area to work with, it can mean removal of parts of the substrate, or simply help with the organisation of the material contained within the piece. Some of the examples we have used to illustrate the various techniques are very dramatic, while some are so simple that they are barely noticed-which underscores the versatility of altering the physical product.

Some format decisions are taken for purely creative reasons, while others are solutions to design problems such as space, size, weight and cost. We hope the examples gathered together in this publication help inspire you in both these aspects.

Client: Sonneti
Design: MadeThought
Process: One-colour
silk-screen print on to
plastic substrate with
reversed-out type

Sonneti:
Autumn/Winter 20
Check it out.
Point 101/Upstairs
Tuesday 10 April

Point 101
Under Centrepoint/
101 New Oxford Street, London W1
Tube: Tottenham Court Road

Sonneti Invite

Paper is by far the most common substrate, but alternatives exist as this invite
designed for Sonneti shows. The design by MadeThought is printed on plastic in a
single colour so that the text is reversed out and see through. The plastic is extremely
flexible, and unlike paper will not crack – particularly useful for an item that will
inevitably have to endure being folded and manhandled.

Client: Scott Perry
Design: Hat-trick
Process: Single-colour,
saddle-stitched mailer with
specially cut pages

...bardofbray.com

is this a trick?

oh, you...

you may touch...

quite dead...

...poses no major threat, quite...

not a sound...

not even breathing

...athetic really, flimsy

...awkward and odd-shaped

it sits there, all vulnerable

now here's a funny thing...

Scott Perry (www.bardofbray.com)
This mailer for copywriter Scott Perry has a series of thin uncoated pages specially
cut as small as a single line.

Format Acknowledgements

Acknowledgements

We would like to thank everyone who supported us during the project including the many art directors, designers and creatives who showed great generosity in allowing us to reproduce their work. Special thanks to everyone that hunted for, collated, compiled and rediscovered some of the fascinating work contained in this book. Thanks to Xavier Young for his patience, determination and skill in photographing the work showcased in this book and to Heather Marshall for modelling. And a final big thanks to Natalia Price-Cabrera – who devised the original concept for this book – Laura Owen, Brian Morris and all the staff at AVA Publishing who never tired of our requests, enquiries and questions, and supported us throughout.

Contacts